# VEGETABLE COOKBOOK FOR VEGETARIANS

# vegetable cookbook for vegetarians

## 200 Recipes from Artichokes to Zucchini

**Lizzie Streit, MS, RDN, LD**

Photography by Thomas J. Story

ROCKRIDGE
PRESS

For general information on our other products and services or to obtain technical support, please contact our Customer Care Department within the U.S. at (866) 744-2665, or outside the U.S. at (510) 253-0500.

Rockridge Press publishes its books in a variety of electronic and print formats. Some content that appears in print may not be available in electronic books, and vice versa.

Interior and Cover Designer: Suzanne LaGasa
Photo Art Director/Art Manager: Meg Baggott
Editor: Myryah Irby
Production Editor: Ashley Polikoff
Photography © 2020 Thomas J. Story. Food styling by Alexa Hyman.

Shutterstock: pp 11, 16, 21, 28, 34, 39, 46, 49, 55, 58, 61, 67, 73, 80, 88, 92, 95, 99, 104, 110, 115, 121, 124, 127, 131, 136, 141, 147, 153, 158, 166, 170, 173, 178, 185, 194, 199, 205, 210, 218, 224, 227, 231, 236, 242, 248, 255, 260, 263, 272.

Author photo courtesy of Allie Bornstein Photography

ISBN: Print 978-1-64739-333-5
eBook 978-1-64739-334-2
R0

*To Will—my husband, best friend, and chief tasting officer.*
*Thank you for your endless support!*

# Contents

# Introduction

I'm Lizzie, a Registered Dietitian who adores vegetables, and I created this cookbook to help you love them, too. In 2013, when my mom and I started receiving a community-supported agriculture (CSA) share at the same time that I was studying to be an RD, I became fascinated with the wonderful world of vegetables. I loved the new types of vegetables that the CSA showed me (turnips, rutabaga, and radicchio, oh my!) and was even more intrigued by the seemingly endless culinary possibilities. Over the last few years of developing vegetable-forward recipes, I've learned how much vegetables can shine as the mainstay of a dish and how they only need simple pantry ingredients to do so.

This cookbook contains 200 vegetable-based meals, sides, and snacks that feature the 50 most popular vegetables. The recipes are fun and flavorful and use basic cooking techniques and ingredients. In part 1, you'll find a handy guide on how to eat with the seasons, a list of the best kitchen equipment and tools to help you prepare more vegetables, and a list to help you stock your pantry for vegetable-forward cooking. Part 2 includes an A-to-Z vegetable index, with information on how to find, select, store, and cook each vegetable, plus two to six recipes per vegetable.

Whether you follow a fully vegetarian diet or you're an omnivore who's interested in eating more vegetables, this book has everything you need. In the following pages, you'll learn just how much every vegetable has to offer and how to make each of them the star of your meals. So, grab that bunch of radishes that always intimidated you at the store or open up your weekly CSA box, and let's get started!

# PART I

# Vegetable Cooking Essentials

Before you browse the assortment of delicious recipes in this book, here is some basic info on getting started in the kitchen with vegetables. From a seasonal vegetable guide to lists of essential cooking tools and pantry staples, this section has everything you need to know about preparing vegetable-forward dishes.

Reference this chapter whenever you need a reminder of what's in season, time-saving tools, and essential ingredients to keep on hand.

# Cooking with the Seasons

There's nothing better than biting into a juicy tomato on a late August afternoon or filling the house with the aroma of autumnal spices as you prepare a squash soup in October. For most home cooks, it's hard to imagine a specific season without the iconic foods that come with that time of year.

A fresher taste is just one benefit of eating vegetables that are in season. Seasonal vegetables are also more accessible and affordable, and they're likely to carry a lower carbon footprint. Asparagus will certainly be the cheapest and most available in the spring compared to the fall. Plus, fresh asparagus travels a shorter distance from the farm to your fork when it's in season, especially if you live close to where it can be grown or you buy it at a farmers' market.

To reap the many benefits of seasonal vegetables, use the following chart to guide your decisions about which recipes to make during a particular time of year. You'll see that most root vegetables and some others are usually available in more than one season, but this will vary depending on growing conditions in your area. I encourage you to take note of when certain vegetables become available at the grocery store, farmers' market, or in your CSA box. The start of a new season means a whole new category of vegetables to explore.

| SPRING | SUMMER | FALL | WINTER |
|--------|--------|------|--------|
| Artichokes | Avocado | Arugula | Beets |
| Arugula | Beets | Beets | Bok Choy |
| Asparagus | Carrots | Bok Choy | Broccoli |
| Avocado | Celery | Broccoli | Broccolini |
| Broccoli | Corn | Broccolini | Broccoli Rabe |
| Broccolini | Cucumbers | Broccoli Rabe | Brussels Sprouts |
| Broccoli Rabe | Eggplant | Brussels Sprouts | Cabbage |
| Cabbage | Garlic | Cabbage | Carrots |

| SPRING | SUMMER | FALL | WINTER |
| --- | --- | --- | --- |
| Carrots | Green Beans | Carrots | Cauliflower and Romanesco |
| Celery | Herbs | Cauliflower and Romanesco | Celery Root |
| Chard | Peppers | Celery | Chard |
| Fava Beans | Shallots | Celery Root | Chicories |
| Garlic | Tomatoes | Chard | Endive |
| Herbs | Watercress | Chicories | Fennel |
| Kohlrabi | Zucchini and Yellow Summer Squash | Endive | Jicama |
| Kale and Other Greens | | Fennel | Kale and Other Greens |
| Lettuce | | Garlic | Kohlrabi |
| Mushrooms | | Ginger | Leeks |
| Onions | | Green Beans | Onions |
| Peas and Peapods | | Herbs | Parsnips |
| Radishes | | Jicama | Potatoes |
| Rhubarb | | Kale and Other Greens | Radishes |
| Spinach | | Kohlrabi | Rutabaga |
| Watercress | | Lettuce | Sweet Potatoes |
| | | Mushrooms | Turnips |
| | | Onions | Winter Squash |
| | | Parsnips | |
| | | Potatoes | |
| | | Rutabaga | |

| SPRING | SUMMER | FALL | WINTER |
|--------|--------|------|--------|
| | | Shallots | |
| | | Spinach | |
| | | Sweet Potatoes | |
| | | Turnips | |
| | | Winter Squash | |

# Kitchen Equipment and Tools

The following tools will make preparing vegetables less daunting and more fun, all while saving you time in the kitchen.

**Blender or immersion blender:** Blenders make it easy to prepare smoothies, dressings, dips, and soups in a flash. And if you really enjoy soups, a handheld immersion blender that lets you blend right in the pot is a game-changing tool.

**Box or hand grater:** Whether it's used to grate vegetables or shred cheese to mix into a recipe, a grater is an essential kitchen tool.

**Chef's knife:** A chef's knife has a sharp, long, broad blade. It's the most versatile tool for preparing vegetables and can be used for all chopping and slicing needs. You can use paring knives for smaller vegetables, but a chef's knife is handy for root vegetables, squash, and other firm produce.

**Citrus squeezer:** A handheld citrus squeezer is used when you need fresh lemon or lime juice for a recipe. It will help you get the most juice possible out of your citrus without making a sticky mess.

**Colander:** Rinse and clean vegetables with ease by placing them in a colander in the sink. A colander is also helpful for draining pasta, beans, and other staples that you may pair with vegetables.

**Food processor:** A food processor isn't necessary to prepare the majority of the recipes in this book, but it can save you a ton of time when making salsas and other dishes that require a lot of chopping.

**Garlic press:** Chopping garlic can be tedious, and it can leave a smell that lingers on your fingers. With a garlic press, you can mince a clove in just a few seconds.

**Mandoline:** This rectangular tool has a sharp blade that can be used to make thin vegetable slices. A mandoline makes more consistent slices than a knife and reduces prep time. It's especially worth getting one if you like to make veggie chips.

**Microplane grater:** Add some extra zest to your recipes with a handheld Microplane grater. The tiny, sharp holes are specifically designed to zest lemons, limes, and oranges.

**Serrated knife:** For some vegetables, it's easier to use a serrated knife with scalloped edges than a straight-bladed chef's knife. Use a serrated knife for produce with soft flesh, such as tomatoes and melons, to cut into them without crushing them.

**Spiralizer:** You can use a spiralizer to make long, stringy "noodles" of zucchini, beets, squash, kohlrabi, sweet potatoes, and more that are fresher and cheaper than the premade ones you might find at the grocery store.

**Steamer basket:** Steaming vegetables in a basket that's placed inside of a pot with a couple of inches of water is one of the easiest ways to prepare them. Most steamer baskets are inexpensive and collapsible for easy storage.

**Swivel peeler:** Whether or not you prefer to peel your vegetables, a swivel peeler is a helpful tool. Use it to peel vegetables with dirty skin, like beets, or make vegetable shavings or ribbons from carrots and parsnips.

**Vegetable brush:** A sturdy brush can be used to scrub away dirt from vegetables. Depending on the vegetable, you may not even need to peel it after you scrub.

# Stocking Your Pantry

Having a well-stocked pantry will help you prepare delicious vegetarian meals at any time without making a special trip to the grocery store. The following staples are foundational ingredients that appear repeatedly in the recipes in this book. They complement and highlight the natural tastes and textures of vegetables to help them shine as the star of your meals.

**Avocado oil:** Although the recipes in this book call for extra-virgin olive oil, you can substitute avocado oil in most cases. Avocado oil has a higher smoke point than olive oil and can be a good option for roasting and cooking vegetables at high heat, whereas extra-virgin olive oil provides the best flavor for dressings and salads.

**Beans:** Dried and canned beans are a filling, protein-packed addition to vegetable-based meals. Stock your pantry with chickpeas, black beans, cannellini (white) beans, lentils, pinto beans, and kidney beans.

**Black pepper:** Pepper is a classic cooking staple, but purchasing whole black peppercorns that you can grind yourself adds the freshest flavor. It can be used to season roasted vegetables or sprinkled onto salads before serving.

**Butter:** Whether it's used to sauté vegetables or as the base for a yummy sauce, butter is a key ingredient to keep on hand. I especially enjoy the richness of grass-fed varieties like Kerrygold and Vital Farms.

**Cheese:** Cheese adds flavor and depth to dishes. My favorite cheeses include aged parmesan, feta, goat, cheddar, gruyère, and gouda. NOTE: Parmesan cheese uses rennet, an enzyme that's found in the lining of a calf's stomach, so it's not technically vegetarian. Other popular cheeses that typically include rennet are Pecorino Romano, Grana Padano, Gorgonzola, Camembert, Emmenthaler, Gruyère, and Manchego. There are some vegetarian versions of these cheeses made with vegetable rennet or microbial enzymes instead, but they can be hard to find. Be sure to check the label if you follow a strict vegetarian diet.

**Citrus:** A simple squeeze of fresh citrus or a sprinkle of zest adds so much to vegetable recipes. Be sure to keep lemons, limes, and oranges on hand. They won't go to waste.

**Extra-virgin olive oil:** A good olive oil is perhaps the single most important ingredient for vegetable-forward meals. You will use it as the base for dressings and marinades, as well as for roasting and sautéing vegetables. Look for olive oils that are labeled extra-virgin and come in a dark glass or metal container, which helps prevent deterioration from exposure to light.

**Flour:** All-purpose flour is essential for vegetable sauces and gravies, as well as for the occasional muffins and cookies that appear in this book.

**Grains and pasta:** Oats, brown rice, quinoa, farro, wild rice, Arborio rice, and pastas (like orzo, penne, and fusilli) make great additions to salads, grain bowls, stir-fries, and Italian-inspired vegetarian dishes.

**Honey and maple syrup:** These sweeteners are used in desserts as well as several salad dressings and roasted vegetable recipes. For the best quality and taste, choose raw, local honeys in glass jars and grade A amber syrups.

**Nuts, seeds, and dried fruit:** Almonds, pecans, walnuts, cashews, sesame seeds, peanuts, peanut butter, raisins, and dried cranberries all make an appearance in several delicious recipes in this book.

**Salt:** The ultimate flavor-booster, salt is key for preparing vegetarian dishes. Kosher or sea salt can be used for most recipes, but pink Himalayan salt and flaky Maldon salt are other favorites.

**Spices and dried herbs:** Some of the most commonly used spices and dried herbs in this book include garlic powder, cinnamon, turmeric, paprika, parsley, basil, oregano, rosemary, and thyme.

**Vinegar:** Similarly to citrus, vinegars contribute acid that helps boost flavor, preserve food, and even improve the appearance of some dishes. My favorites include apple cider, red wine, balsamic, and rice vinegars.

**Yogurt:** Several recipes call for Greek yogurt as a substitute for mayonnaise or heavy cream. Choose full-fat Greek yogurt or Icelandic skyr, such as Siggi's brand, for maximum creaminess and rich flavor.

**Other flavorings:** Some other canned and bottled goods that add flavor to vegetarian recipes include canned tomatoes, soy sauce, toasted sesame oil, vegetable broth, canned coconut milk, Dijon mustard, capers, canned chipotle peppers in adobo, salsa, and sriracha and other hot sauces.

# PART II

# The Vegetables and Recipes

Simple Steamed Artichokes, Page 12

# Artichokes

**Season:** spring

**Flavor profile:** Artichokes are a type of thistle with beautiful green, edible outer leaves that surround a tender "heart." The heart sits on top of the stem and a fuzzy, inedible center called a "choke." Artichokes have a rich flavor that's earthy and slightly sweet, and the heart is considered the most flavorful and meaty part.

**Pairs with:** lemon, butter, creamy sauces made with mayonnaise or yogurt, parmesan cheese, fresh herbs, garlic

**Varieties:** globe (most popular, also known as round), baby (no fuzzy chokes!), purple (several varieties)

**Preparation:** To prepare artichokes for cooking, have a serrated or sharp knife, fresh lemon wedges, and kitchen scissors handy. Once cooked, you can eat the artichoke by removing the leaves and using your teeth to scrape away the tender flesh. Discard the tougher leaves after eating the flesh, but eat the heart whole.

**Favorite ways to serve:** roasted, steamed, braised

**Nutritional info:** Artichokes are high in vitamin C, magnesium, and inulin,

a dietary fiber that acts as a prebiotic and can feed healthy gut bacteria.

**Selection:** Look for artichokes that are heavy with tight leaves that have not opened. To test an artichoke's freshness, give it a firm squeeze. If it squeaks, you have a fresh one.

**Storage:** Store raw artichokes in a plastic bag poked with a few holes in the refrigerator for five to seven days. Cooked artichokes are best eaten right away but can last in an airtight container in the refrigerator for a few days.

# Simple Steamed Artichokes

**SERVES 4 / PREP TIME:** 10 minutes / **COOK TIME:** 35 minutes

**4 fresh artichokes**

**1 lemon, quartered**

1. Using a sharp or serrated knife, cut off about ½ inch from both the top and the stem of each artichoke. Remove the tough outer leaves toward the bottom. Use kitchen scissors to snip the pointy tops off the other leaves. Rub the cut surfaces with the lemon to prevent browning.

2. Fill a large pot with a few inches of water, and squeeze some lemon juice into it.

3. Place a steamer basket inside the pot, and put the artichokes in the basket. If you don't have a basket, put the artichokes directly into the pot, stem-side up. Bring to a boil over high heat.

4. Reduce the heat to medium-low. Cover, and simmer for 25 to 35 minutes. The artichokes are finished cooking when the heart is fork-tender and you can easily peel off the leaves. Remove from the heat.

5. Enjoy a freshly steamed artichoke by dipping a leaf into a sauce of your choice (see notes in Roasted Artichokes with Lemon Butter on page 14 for options) and using your teeth to scrape away the tender flesh. The heart and stem are also edible, but the fuzzy choke should be discarded.

# Marinated Artichoke Hearts

**SERVES 4 / PREP TIME:** 5 minutes, plus 2 hours to chill

*The heart of an artichoke is the most flavorful part, and this simple recipe helps boost that delicious taste even more. You can reserve the hearts of freshly steamed artichokes for this recipe or use canned artichoke hearts. Serve these Italian-inspired treats on top of pasta, on charcuterie and vegetable platters, or straight out of the jar.*

**1 (14-ounce) can artichoke hearts in water, drained, rinsed, and quartered, or 2 cups steamed artichoke hearts, quartered**

**½ cup extra-virgin olive oil**

**¼ cup apple cider vinegar**

**2 garlic cloves, thinly sliced**

**1 teaspoon dried oregano**

**½ teaspoon salt**

**Pinch red pepper flakes**

1. Put the artichoke hearts in a glass jar with a lid.

2. In a small bowl, whisk together the olive oil, vinegar, garlic, oregano, salt, and red pepper flakes.

3. Pour the mixture over the artichokes, seal the lid, and gently shake. Refrigerate for at least 2 hours before serving.

NOTE: You can substitute white wine vinegar or red wine vinegar for apple cider vinegar, or use the same amount of lemon juice instead. Feel free to get creative with your seasonings. Fresh thyme sprigs, whole peppercorns, and more red pepper flakes would be great additions. Marinated artichokes can be stored for up to two weeks in the refrigerator.

# Roasted Artichokes with Lemon Butter

**SERVES 4** / **PREP TIME:** 10 minutes / **COOK TIME:** 50 minutes

*Roasting artichokes brings out their incredible flavor and transforms their leaves from tough to melt-in-your-mouth tender. For an added bonus, save the roasted garlic cloves that were stuffed into each artichoke to mix into the lemon butter. This will elevate your dip from delicious to decadent.*

## FOR THE ARTICHOKES

**2 tablespoons extra-virgin olive oil, divided**
**4 fresh artichokes**
**1 lemon, quartered**
**4 to 8 garlic cloves, peeled**
**Fresh thyme sprigs**
**Salt**
**Freshly ground black pepper**

## FOR THE LEMON BUTTER

**Juice of 1 lemon**
**4 tablespoons (½ stick) salted butter, melted**

## TO MAKE THE ARTICHOKES

1. Preheat the oven to 400°F. Drizzle a 9-by-13-inch baking dish with 1 tablespoon of olive oil.

2. Using a sharp or serrated knife, cut off about ½ inch from both the top and the stem of each artichoke. Remove the tough outer leaves toward the bottom. Use kitchen scissors to snip the pointy tops off the other leaves. Rub the cut surfaces with the lemon to prevent browning. Cut each artichoke in half, rub the cut surfaces with the lemon again, and use a spoon to remove the fuzzy choke.

3. Put the artichokes in the prepared baking dish.

4. Stuff each artichoke with 1 or 2 garlic cloves and thyme sprigs. Drizzle with the remaining 1 tablespoon of olive oil. Season with salt and pepper.

5. Carefully flip each artichoke over, ensuring that the garlic clove stays in the middle. Season with salt and pepper. Cover the baking dish with foil.

6. Transfer the baking dish to the oven, and bake for 40 to 50 minutes, or until the artichoke leaves are tender and can be easily removed. Remove from the oven.

**TO MAKE THE LEMON BUTTER**

7. A few minutes before the artichokes are finished cooking, in a small bowl, mix together the lemon juice and butter. Add the tender roasted garlic cloves, if desired.

8. To serve, remove a leaf, dip in the lemon butter, and use your teeth to scrape off the tender part of the leaf.

NOTE: Other dipping sauce options include a mix of ½ cup mayonnaise, some lemon juice, and 2 to 3 minced garlic cloves or a mix of ½ cup plain Greek yogurt with salt and fresh thyme, parsley, and chives.

# Arugula

**Season:** spring, fall

**Flavor profile:** Arugula, also known as rocket, is a leafy green vegetable with a slightly spicy, peppery taste. It has hints of nuts and mustard and can be used as both a salad green and an herb.

**Pairs with:** olive oil, balsamic vinegar, lemon, parmesan cheese, almonds, pine nuts, sunflower seeds, pears, apples, oranges, bell peppers

**Varieties:** common arugula (mostly found in the United States) and wild arugula (mostly found in Europe)

**Preparation:** Remove any wilted or yellow leaves. Wash arugula under cold water, and pat dry with a clean towel before cooking.

**Favorite ways to serve:** raw in salads and condiments, sautéed

**Nutritional info:** Arugula is an excellent source of vitamin K, a fat-soluble nutrient that's necessary for blood clotting. It also contains vitamin C, calcium, iron, and potassium.

**Selection:** Choose fresh arugula that has bright green leaves without yellow edges, wilting, or holes. Baby arugula has a milder and less bitter taste than bigger leaves that are left on the stem longer.

**Storage:** Wash and dry arugula before placing it between paper towels. Store in a plastic bag or airtight container in the refrigerator. Depending on how fresh it was when you got it, arugula can last for up to 10 days.

# Lemony Arugula and Parmesan Salad

**SERVES 4 / PREP TIME:** 5 minutes

**2 tablespoons extra-virgin olive oil**

**1 tablespoon freshly squeezed lemon juice**

**4 to 6 cups loosely packed arugula**

**¼ cup shaved vegetarian parmesan cheese**

1. In a large bowl, whisk together the olive oil and lemon juice.

2. Add the arugula and parmesan cheese. Toss to combine.

# Arugula Salsa Verde

**MAKES 2 CUPS** / **PREP TIME:** 15 minutes / **COOK TIME:** 5 to 10 minutes

*In Italian tradition, salsa verde ("green sauce") is made with fresh parsley, garlic, onion, capers, and anchovies, whereas Mexican salsa verde features tomatillos, garlic, onion, cilantro, lime, and hot peppers. This recipe combines flavors from both types, resulting in something quite new. Though it may seem like a traditional Mexican salsa verde, it gets a peppery kick from one of the most loved greens in Italian cuisine—arugula.*

**1 pound tomatillos, husked and rinsed**

**3 cups loosely packed arugula**

**1 jalapeño pepper, seeded and finely chopped**

**½ cup diced red onion**

**2 garlic cloves, minced, plus more as needed**

**¼ cup chopped fresh cilantro, plus more as needed**

**Juice of 1 lime, plus more as needed**

**½ teaspoon salt, plus more as needed**

1. Turn the broiler to high. Line a baking sheet with aluminum foil or parchment paper.

2. Put the tomatillos on the prepared baking sheet.

3. Transfer the baking sheet to the oven, and broil for 5 to 7 minutes, or until the skins are lightly blackened. Remove from the oven.

4. Transfer the tomatillos and their juices to a food processor or blender.

5. Add the arugula, jalapeño, onion, garlic, cilantro, lime juice, and salt. Pulse for 30 to 60 seconds, or until the salsa is finely chopped. Taste, and add more salt, lime juice, garlic, or cilantro as needed.

**NOTE:** Store the salsa in an airtight container in the refrigerator for up to 2 weeks. It will thicken the longer it is stored. For a milder salsa, use half of the jalapeño, or omit it altogether. For more spice, add another jalapeño or more arugula. Serve with tortilla chips, on top of tacos or burritos, or mixed into guacamole.

# Sautéed Arugula with Roasted Red Peppers

**SERVES 4** / **PREP TIME:** 5 minutes / **COOK TIME:** 10 minutes

*Sweet bell peppers complement spicy arugula in this easy side dish, and making the roasted red peppers in advance saves tons of time. Enjoy this dish alongside pasta, serve it on top of toasted bread, or bulk it up with white beans for a main dish. However you enjoy this recipe, be sure to add a drizzle of balsamic vinegar before serving for a burst of flavor.*

**1 tablespoon extra-virgin olive oil**

**3 garlic cloves, minced**

**6 cups loosely packed arugula**

**1 cup Roasted Red Peppers** (page 206)

**Salt**

**Freshly ground black pepper**

**Balsamic vinegar, for serving**

1. In a large skillet, warm the olive oil over medium heat.

2. Add the garlic and cook for 1 to 2 minutes, or until fragrant.

3. Add the arugula and cook, stirring occasionally, for 2 to 3 minutes, or until beginning to wilt.

4. Add the red peppers and cook, stirring, for a few more minutes. Season with salt and pepper to taste. Remove from the heat. Drizzle with vinegar just before serving.

**NOTE:** Arugula cooks down quickly, so use more if you have a lot on hand. Possible additions include red pepper flakes, mushrooms, fresh parsley, and onion.

# Sunflower Seed and Arugula Pesto

**MAKES ABOUT 2 CUPS / PREP TIME:** 10 minutes

*Arugula's potent flavor makes it a versatile ingredient that can be used like fresh herbs. This nontraditional pesto features arugula alongside sunflower seeds and gouda cheese. It has a vibrant green color and a salty, spicy, and nutty taste that is delicious as a vegetable dip or on sandwiches, pasta, pizzas, and eggs. If you're swimming in arugula, this recipe is for you. You can easily double or triple it and freeze the leftovers.*

**2 cups packed arugula leaves**

**½ cup raw or dry-roasted sunflower seeds**

**Juice of ½ lemon**

**1 garlic clove, minced**

**½ cup grated vegetarian gouda cheese**

**½ cup extra-virgin olive oil, plus more for drizzling**

**Salt**

1. In a food processor or high-powered blender, combine the arugula, sunflower seeds, lemon juice, garlic, and gouda cheese.

2. Slowly add the olive oil through the small hole in the top while you pulse for 30 to 60 seconds, or until smooth. Using a rubber spatula, scrape down the sides as needed. You may also need a few more drizzles of olive oil to blend to the desired consistency. Season with salt to taste.

**NOTE:** Store in an airtight container in the refrigerator for up to 2 weeks. You can freeze pesto in small containers, ice cube trays, or muffin tins for a few hours before transferring it to a plastic bag for later use. If desired, substitute walnuts or pine nuts for the sunflower seeds and parmesan for gouda for a more traditional pesto.

# Asparagus

**Season:** spring

**Flavor profile:** Asparagus is a spear-like vegetable with pointy, scaly tips. It is a member of the lily family and comes in a variety of colors. Fresh asparagus has a mild, earthy taste but can taste bitter or sour when overcooked. Its mellow flavor allows it to soak up other flavors and seasonings particularly well.

**Pairs with:** garlic, lemon, tarragon, mint, dill, soy, sesame, balsamic vinegar, salty cheeses

**Varieties:** green (garden), purple, white

**Preparation:** Rinse asparagus under water, and snap off or trim the bottom of the spears with a knife to remove any woody or discolored parts.

**Favorite ways to serve:** shaved, steamed, sautéed, roasted

**Nutritional info:** Asparagus contains fiber, potassium, and vitamins A, C, E, and K. It is particularly high in folate, which is an important nutrient for expectant moms due to its role in promoting healthy fetal development.

**Selection:** Look for asparagus that has firm stalks with tightly closed tips and few woody ends. Thin asparagus spears taste especially good in roasted and

sautéed dishes, while thicker stalks work well for shaved preparations, pastas, risottos, and soups.

**Storage:** Fill a glass jar with a couple of inches of water, and store the asparagus spears upright in the refrigerator for up to four days. Or wrap the ends with a damp paper towel, and place the bunch in a perforated plastic bag.

# Roasted Asparagus

**SERVES 4** / **PREP TIME:** 5 minutes / **COOK TIME:** 15 minutes

**1 pound asparagus (about 1 bunch), trimmed**

**1 teaspoon extra-virgin olive oil**

**Salt**

**Freshly ground black pepper**

1. Preheat the oven to 400°F. Line a baking sheet with aluminum foil or parchment paper.

2. On the prepared baking sheet, using your hands or a rubber spatula, toss the asparagus with the olive oil until lightly coated. Season with salt and pepper to taste.

3. Arrange the asparagus in an even layer.

4. Transfer the baking sheet to the oven and roast for 12 to 15 minutes, or until the spears are tender and crisp. Remove from the oven.

NOTE: Additional seasoning options include garlic powder, red pepper flakes, lemon zest or juice, and chopped fresh herbs.

# Shaved Asparagus and Pine Nut Salad

**SERVES 4 / PREP TIME:** 15 minutes / **COOK TIME:** 5 minutes

*Raw asparagus is a true springtime treat. It's sweet, mild, and downright delicious. Shaved asparagus is also a beautiful style of presentation. This simple side is easy enough for a weeknight meal and elegant enough to impress guests at a spring-inspired dinner. Before you get started, have a swivel peeler or sharp paring knife on hand to make the signature "ribbons" for this salad.*

### FOR THE SALAD

**1 pound asparagus (about 1 bunch), trimmed**

**¼ cup pine nuts**

### FOR THE DRESSING

**2 tablespoons extra-virgin olive oil**

**1 teaspoon Dijon mustard**

**1 tablespoon freshly squeezed lemon juice**

**Salt**

**Freshly ground black pepper**

### TO MAKE THE SALAD

1. Lay the asparagus flat on a cutting board. Using one hand, hold a spear down while you use the other to make long shavings with a vegetable peeler or knife. There will be some uneven pieces, especially as you get toward the end of the stalk, but don't throw them out. You can cut them into smaller pieces and add them to the salad. Put the shaved asparagus in a bowl.

2. In a skillet, toast the pine nuts over medium heat, stirring frequently, for 2 to 3 minutes, or until fragrant. Remove from the heat. Add the nuts to the asparagus.

### TO MAKE THE DRESSING

3. In a separate bowl, whisk together the olive oil, mustard, and lemon juice. Season with salt and pepper to taste.

4. Add the dressing to the asparagus, and toss to combine. Season with salt and pepper to taste.

# Baked Asparagus Fries

**SERVES 4 / PREP TIME:** 15 minutes **/ COOK TIME:** 15 minutes

*Long and lanky asparagus make for the perfect fries. With a simple coating of bread crumbs, parmesan cheese, and garlic powder, you won't believe how quickly this crunchy snack comes together. Asparagus fries provide a healthy dose of nutrients while satisfying a craving for comfort food. Try them on a chilly April day—they will fill you up and get you in the mood for more seasonal vegetables.*

**½ cup all-purpose flour**

**2 large eggs, beaten**

**1 cup bread crumbs**

**½ cup grated vegetarian parmesan cheese**

**1 teaspoon garlic powder**

**¼ teaspoon salt**

**1 pound asparagus (about 1 bunch), trimmed**

1. Preheat the oven to 425°F. Line a baking sheet with parchment paper.

2. Prepare 3 shallow bowls as follows: one with the flour, one with the eggs, and one with a mixture of the bread crumbs, parmesan cheese, garlic powder, and salt.

3. Roll each asparagus spear in the flour, followed by the eggs, and finally in the bread crumb and cheese mixture, making sure that each asparagus spear is fully coated in each bowl's ingredients before moving on to the next. If you find that the flour is not sticking, rinse the asparagus and gently shake off some of the water (to leave a few droplets) before rolling it in the flour.

4. Arrange the asparagus in a single layer on the prepared baking sheet.

5. Transfer the baking sheet to the oven and bake for 12 to 15 minutes, flipping halfway through, or until the asparagus is crispy and slightly browned. Remove from the oven.

**NOTE:** Serve these fries with a dipping sauce, such as ½ cup Greek yogurt mixed with 1 tablespoon lemon juice, 1 tablespoon chopped fresh dill, and salt to taste or a mixture of ½ cup mayonnaise, 1 minced garlic clove, and 1 teaspoon smoked paprika.

# Asparagus and Quinoa Egg Muffins

**MAKES 12 MUFFINS** / **PREP TIME:** 10 minutes / **COOK TIME:** 35 minutes

*Egg muffins are a great on-the-go breakfast that you can prep ahead of time. The asparagus and chives give them a bright flavor, while quinoa provides a boost of protein and fiber. Grab a couple before you head out the door in the morning, pour yourself coffee while they reheat, and start your day with a dose of delicious vegetables.*

**Nonstick cooking spray**

**1 tablespoon extra-virgin olive oil**

**½ cup diced yellow onion**

**2 cups diced asparagus**

**1 cup cooked quinoa**

**¼ cup chopped fresh chives**

**¾ cup crumbled vegetarian feta cheese**

**8 large eggs, plus 1 to 2 more as needed**

**Salt**

**Freshly ground black pepper**

1. Preheat the oven to 350°F. Generously coat a 12-cup muffin tin with cooking spray.

2. In a large skillet, warm the olive oil over medium heat.

3. Add the onion and asparagus. Sauté for 5 to 7 minutes, or until slightly tender. Remove from the heat.

4. Stir in the quinoa, chives, and feta cheese. Spoon the mixture equally into each cup of the muffin tin.

5. In a separate bowl or a large measuring cup, whisk the eggs. Season with salt and pepper to taste. Pour on top of the vegetables and quinoa; fill each cup close to the top, being careful not to overflow. If you need more eggs, beat 1 or 2 more, and add them.

CONTINUED

6.  Transfer the muffin tin to the oven and bake for 20 to 25 minutes, or until the eggs have set in the middle. Remove from the oven. Let cool for just a couple minutes before carefully transferring each muffin to a wire rack to finish cooling.

NOTE: The cooking time of this recipe does not include cooking the quinoa, which can be prepped in advance to save time. Be sure to spray the muffin tin very well to prevent sticking. You can also use silicone or parchment paper muffin liners, but regular paper liners will not work because the muffins will stick to them. Store the muffins in an airtight container in the refrigerator for up to 5 days. Reheat in the microwave on high for 1 to 2 minutes. You can also freeze the muffins in a zip-top plastic bag for up to 3 months. Thaw in the refrigerator overnight before reheating.

# Asparagus Soup with Peas

**SERVES 4 / PREP TIME:** 10 minutes / **COOK TIME:** 30 minutes

*This vibrant soup is like spring in a bowl. With the addition of green peas and the use of protein-rich Greek yogurt instead of heavy cream, it's super nutritious without sacrificing flavor. I've added the peas after blending to give texture. Though this soup is tasty enough on its own, a thick piece of crunchy bread for dipping makes it even better.*

**1 tablespoon extra-virgin olive oil**

**1 sweet onion, diced**

**2 garlic cloves, minced**

**Salt**

**Freshly ground black pepper**

**1 pound asparagus (about 1 bunch), trimmed and cut into 1-inch pieces**

**4 cups vegetable broth**

**1 cup frozen or fresh peas**

**2 tablespoons chopped fresh dill, plus more for serving**

**½ cup full-fat plain Greek yogurt, plus more for serving**

1. In a large pot or Dutch oven, warm the olive oil over medium heat.

2. Add the onion and garlic. Sauté for 3 to 4 minutes, or until soft. Season with salt and pepper.

3. Add the asparagus and broth. Stir to combine.

4. Increase the heat to high. Cover and bring to a boil.

5. Reduce the heat to medium-low. Cook for 20 to 25 minutes, or until the asparagus is fork-tender. Season with salt and pepper to taste. Remove from the heat.

6. Using an immersion blender, puree the soup.

7. Add the peas, dill, and yogurt. Stir to combine. Cook over medium heat for 3 to 5 minutes, or until the soup is warmed through and the peas are tender. Remove from the heat.

8. Serve the soup with more dill and a dollop of Greek yogurt.

**NOTE:** You can also use a regular blender for this recipe. To do this safely, fill the blender halfway, and puree the soup in batches. Leave a corner of the lid cracked, or remove the top of the blender and cover it with a folded dish towel to let steam escape as you blend. Be careful not to get burned by the steam. Transfer the soup back to the pot, and continue with the rest of the recipe. To make it vegan, omit the yogurt or use plant-based yogurt.

# Avocado

**Season:** spring, summer

**Flavor profile:** Avocados have creamy, bright green flesh with a brown pit and black or green skin. Botanically, they're considered a fruit, but they're typically eaten as a vegetable. Avocados have a rich, earthy, and slightly sweet flavor and contribute a buttery texture to dips, sauces, and smoothies.

**Pairs with:** lime and lemon juice, garlic, onion, spicy peppers, beans, chocolate, honey, and salty cheeses like cotija, parmesan, and feta

**Varieties:** Hass (sourced from Mexico and California), fuerte (green skin), Florida (also known as Dominican, with green skin, larger pits, and lower fat content), as well as several other types that range from pear-shaped to oval

**Preparation:** Cut an avocado in half lengthwise from stem to end, rotating it with one hand while keeping your knife steady with the other. Twist the avocado open with your hands, tap the knife firmly into the pit, and twist the knife to dislodge it. Scoop the flesh out with a spoon.

**Favorite ways to serve:** mashed into guacamole, served on toast and in salads

**Nutritional info:** Avocados are known for being high in heart-healthy mono-unsaturated fats, but they are also a source of potassium and magnesium, which help maintain healthy blood pressure.

**Selection:** To figure out if an avocado is ripe, gently press your thumb into the skin. It should feel soft but not mushy. The skin of Hass avocados gets darker as they ripen, but this does not happen with most other varieties.

**Storage:** Unripe avocados should be stored on the countertop for up to six days until ripe, then transferred to the refrigerator for up to four days. To store half of an avocado for later use, brush the flesh with lemon juice or olive oil to prevent browning, tightly wrap with plastic wrap, and refrigerate.

# Avocado-Lime Mash

**SERVES 4** / **PREP TIME:** 5 minutes

*Try adding chopped cilantro, bell peppers, onion, or tomatoes (or a mixture of them) to vary the flavor of this recipe. This mash should be made right before serving because it doesn't store well and will turn brown.*

**4 ripe avocados**
**Juice of 2 limes**
**Salt**
**Tortilla chips or toast,**
  **for serving**

1. Using a sharp knife, cut each avocado in half lengthwise from stem to end, rotating it with one hand while holding the knife with the other to cut the entire fruit. Using your hands, open the avocado, press your knife firmly into the pit, and twist the knife to remove it. Cut the flesh crosswise and lengthwise to make cubes, and use a spoon to scoop it into a bowl.

2. Add the lime juice. Season with salt to taste. Using the back of a fork, mash the avocado.

3. Serve the mash with tortilla chips, or spread it onto toast.

# Baked Eggs in Avocado

**SERVES 4 / PREP TIME:** 5 minutes / **COOK TIME:** 20 minutes

*Made with only two ingredients, this recipe is a tried-and-true favorite for breakfast or dinner. Rich avocado is a delicious companion to runny eggs, and keeping the skin on makes it easy to eat and clean up. Loaded with brain-boosting healthy fats and protein, this dish is also completely customizable. Add your favorite shredded cheese, herbs, salsa, or pesto before you dig in.*

**2 ripe avocados, halved lengthwise and pitted**
**4 large eggs**

1. Preheat the oven to 425°F.

2. Using a spoon, scoop out 1 to 2 tablespoons of the flesh from the center of each avocado to create a wider circle for the eggs to sit in.

3. Place the avocado halves in a baking dish so they stay upright or on top of ramekins placed on a baking sheet.

4. Carefully crack 1 egg into the hole of each avocado half.

5. Transfer the baking dish to the oven, and bake for 15 to 20 minutes, or until the egg whites have set but the yolks are still runny (or to your desired consistency). Remove from the oven.

**NOTE:** Some of the egg whites may spill over the sides of the avocados. They will still turn out fine if this happens, but you can also crack the egg into a bowl, spoon the yolk into each avocado half, and then add just enough of the egg white to fill the rest of the hole.

# Pineapple-Avocado Salad

**SERVES 4 / PREP TIME:** 15 minutes

*Creamy avocados complement pineapple and serrano pepper in this warm weather dish. Even though it's made with simple ingredients, the sweet, spicy, and cooling tastes, plus a touch of fresh dill, provide a variety of interesting flavors. You can serve it as a side as part of a summer cookout, eat it with tortilla chips, or add it to tacos and burrito bowls. Or, add some black beans to make it a complete meal.*

**FOR THE DRESSING**

Juice of 2 limes
2 teaspoons honey

**FOR THE SALAD**

2 ripe avocados, halved
  lengthwise and pitted
3 cups diced pineapple
1 cup diced red onion
1 small serrano
  pepper, seeded and
  finely chopped
3 tablespoons chopped
  fresh dill
Salt

**TO MAKE THE DRESSING**

1.  In a large bowl, whisk together the lime juice and honey.

**TO MAKE THE SALAD**

2.  Cut the avocado flesh into cubes, and use a spoon to scoop it into the bowl.

3.  Add the pineapple, onion, serrano pepper, and dill. Stir to combine. Season with salt to taste.

**NOTE:** Use a jalapeño pepper instead of a serrano pepper for less heat, or omit the pepper entirely. You can also substitute fresh cilantro for the dill.

# Avocado Toast with Quick Pickled Red Onions

**SERVES 4 / PREP TIME:** 5 minutes

*When my husband and I visited Australia for our honeymoon, we fell in love with their take on avocado toast. Most restaurants served it on sourdough bread with pickled red onions, and sometimes they added sweet corn, crumbled feta, or an Egyptian and Middle Eastern spice blend called dukkah, made with crushed nuts and seeds. Aussie-inspired avocado toast is now one of my favorite dishes to make for "brekkie." It tastes especially delicious alongside a cappuccino dusted with shaved chocolate, another Australian specialty.*

**2 ripe avocados, halved lengthwise and pitted**

**4 large sourdough bread slices, toasted**

**½ cup Quick Pickled Red Onions** (page 192)

**¼ cup hemp seeds**

**½ cup crumbled vegetarian feta cheese**

1. Scoop the flesh out of the avocados. Using a fork, mash it on top of each slice of bread.

2. Divide the pickled onions, hemp seeds, and feta cheese equally among the toasts.

**NOTE:** If you can find dukkah at the store, add a sprinkle to the toast, or use it instead of the hemp seeds. It is so delicious! You can also add corn, chopped cherry tomatoes, a poached egg, or all three, and substitute rye or multigrain toast for the sourdough.

# Parmesan Crisps with Lemony Avocado

**SERVES 4** / **PREP TIME:** 10 minutes / **COOK TIME:** 5 minutes

*Fresh avocado tossed in lemon juice tastes delicious on top of parmesan cheese crisps. These bite-size snacks are equal parts salty, creamy, and zesty—they go down easy. Ready in 15 minutes, loaded parmesan crisps make for an easy appetizer for a party or a yummy after-school or post-work snack. Be sure to use freshly grated parmesan cheese, instead of buying it pre-grated, for best results.*

**1 cup freshly grated vegetarian parmesan cheese**
**1 ripe avocado, halved lengthwise and pitted**
**Juice of ½ lemon**
**Chopped fresh cilantro leaves, for garnish**

1. Preheat the oven to 400°F. Line a baking sheet with parchment paper.

2. Using a tablespoon, scoop out 12 even piles of parmesan cheese onto the prepared baking sheet, leaving 1 to 2 inches between them.

3. Transfer the baking sheet to the center rack of the oven, and bake for 4 to 6 minutes, or until the edges are bubbling and golden. Remove from the oven. Let cool for a few minutes to crisp up even more.

4. Cut the avocado flesh into cubes and use a spoon to scoop it into a bowl.

5. Add the lemon juice and toss.

6. Spoon the avocado onto the crisps and garnish each with a cilantro leaf. Serve right away.

NOTE: Keep a close eye on the parmesan crisps so that they don't get too brown, which will make them taste bitter. You can easily double or triple this recipe for larger groups, but you should make one batch of crisps at a time. This way, they can always be placed on the center rack of the oven for even cooking.

# Beans

**Season:** spring, summer, fall, winter

**Flavor profile:** Beans are the seeds found inside pods of plants from the legume family. Although they are not technically vegetables, beans are a common addition to vegetarian meals. The flavor of beans differs from one to the next, but most varieties have a mild, earthy taste and creamy texture. As such, they can easily soak up added flavors and seasonings.

**Pairs with:** soups, tacos, salads, peppers, onion, garlic, cumin, paprika, chili powder, lime

**Varieties:** black, pinto, kidney, navy, soy, cannellini (white), chickpeas (garbanzo), and lentils

**Preparation:** Canned cooked beans are widely available. Drain and rinse under cold water before using. You can also prepare dried beans on the stovetop and in a slow cooker or pressure cooker.

**Favorite ways to serve:** cooked in broth and spices for maximum flavor, blended into dips, roasted

**Nutritional info:** The nutritional content of beans is different for each variety, but they are all generally high in fiber and plant-based protein. Chickpeas, pinto beans, and black beans are also rich in essential nutrients like folate, iron, and manganese.

**Selection:** Canned beans do not differ in taste and texture across brands but do contain varying amounts of sodium. If you are watching your salt intake, choose low-sodium or no-salt-added varieties. For dried beans, look for packages that are tightly sealed with no shriveled or broken beans.

**Storage:** Cooked beans can be stored in an airtight container in the refrigerator for up to five days. Prior to cooking, store dried beans in tightly sealed containers in a cool, dry place.

# Easy Stovetop Black Beans

**SERVES 4** / **PREP TIME:** 5 minutes, plus overnight to soak / **COOK TIME:** 1 hour 5 minutes

**1 cup dried black beans**

**1 teaspoon salt**

**1 bay leaf**

1. Inspect the beans, and discard any shriveled or broken ones.

2. In a large bowl, combine the beans with 8 cups of water. Soak overnight at room temperature.

3. Drain and rinse the beans. Put in a large pot with 4 cups of water, the salt, and bay leaf. Bring to a gentle boil over medium-high heat. Cover, reduce the heat to low, and cook for 45 minutes to 1 hour, or until the beans are tender. Remove from the heat.

# Cumin-Lime Three Bean Salad

**SERVES 6** / **PREP TIME:** 15 minutes

*An easy bean dish is a versatile staple to have in your cooking repertoire. This potluck-ready three bean salad features Southwest ingredients, and it's loaded with fiber and plant-based protein, making it a filling vegetarian main dish that's bound to become a go-to recipe. Enjoy it on its own, nestled into tacos, or on top of brown rice.*

## FOR THE DRESSING

¼ cup extra-virgin olive oil

Juice of 2 limes

1 tablespoon ground cumin, plus more as needed

¾ teaspoon sea salt, plus more as needed

## FOR THE SALAD

1 (15-ounce) can kidney beans, drained and rinsed

1 (15-ounce) can black beans, drained and rinsed

1 (15-ounce) can pinto beans, drained and rinsed

1 (15-ounce) can sweet corn, drained and rinsed

1 red bell pepper, seeded and diced

## TO MAKE THE DRESSING

1. In a large bowl, whisk together the olive oil, lime juice, cumin, and salt.

## TO MAKE THE SALAD

2. Add the kidney beans, black beans, pinto beans, corn, and bell pepper. Toss to combine. Taste and adjust the seasonings as needed. Cover with plastic wrap and refrigerate for 30 minutes before serving.

**NOTE:** This salad tastes best after sitting for at least 30 minutes in the refrigerator, but it can be served immediately. Possible additions include chopped fresh cilantro, crumbled vegetarian feta cheese, chopped red onion, or jalapeño pepper slices. Store leftovers in an airtight container in the refrigerator for up to 5 days.

# Paprika-Roasted Chickpeas

**SERVES 4** / **PREP TIME:** 5 minutes / **COOK TIME:** 30 minutes

*Roasted chickpeas are a healthy, delicious way to satisfy a snack attack. Smoked paprika contributes a smoky yet sweet flavor that nicely complements mild, earthy chickpeas. I enjoy eating them on their own, but you can also add roasted chickpeas to salads and soups. In any case, this recipe will be way cheaper than store-bought chips, crackers, and other crunchy snacks.*

**1 (15-ounce) can chickpeas, drained and rinsed**

**1 tablespoon extra-virgin olive oil**

**1 teaspoon smoked paprika**

**¼ teaspoon sea salt**

1. Preheat the oven to 400°F. Line a baking sheet with foil or parchment paper.

2. Pat the chickpeas dry with paper towels.

3. In a medium bowl, mix together the olive oil, paprika, and salt.

4. Add the chickpeas, and toss until well coated.

5. Spread the chickpeas out in an even layer on the prepared baking sheet.

6. Transfer the baking sheet to the oven, and roast for 25 to 30 minutes, checking after 15 minutes to avoid burning and to shake the baking sheet, or until the chickpeas are crispy. Remove from the oven. Let cool for a few minutes before eating.

**NOTE:** These chickpeas are crispiest right after they are roasted. They will get softer the longer they sit out, but they will still taste delicious. Store leftovers in an airtight container at room temperature for up to 5 days. Other possible seasonings include garlic powder, curry powder, or cayenne pepper.

# Creamy White Bean Dip

**MAKES ABOUT 1½ CUPS / PREP TIME:** 5 minutes

*Cannellini beans, also known as white beans, are one of the creamiest legumes. Their smooth texture lends itself well to dips and spreads, but that's not even the best part. With just a few other pantry ingredients, you can prepare this fiber-rich snack in 5 minutes flat. Serve it with carrot sticks, pita chips, or seed crackers, and use it as a spread on toast or sandwiches.*

**1 (15-ounce) can cannellini beans, drained and rinsed**
**2 garlic cloves, minced**
**Juice of ½ lemon, plus more as needed**
**1 tablespoon fresh thyme leaves, plus more for serving**
**¼ cup extra-virgin olive oil, plus more for drizzling**
**Salt**

1. In a food processor or high-powered blender, combine the beans, garlic, lemon juice, thyme, and olive oil. Pulse for 30 to 60 seconds, or until smooth. Add about 1 tablespoon of water as needed to promote blending. Season with salt and more lemon juice to taste.

2. Serve the dip in a small bowl with a drizzle of olive oil and fresh thyme leaves.

**NOTE:** Feel free to substitute fresh oregano or rosemary for the thyme. For a spicy kick, add a pinch of red pepper flakes or cayenne pepper. You can also use Great Northern or navy beans for this recipe.

# Beets

**Season:** summer, fall, winter

**Flavor profile:** Beets are hearty root vegetables known for their earthy yet slightly sweet flavor. Raw beets have a more pronounced earthiness, whereas cooked beets taste sweeter. Beet greens are also edible and taste similar to other dark, leafy greens.

**Pairs with:** savory herbs, tart cheeses like goat cheese, walnuts, almonds, pistachios, pecans, honey, chocolate

**Varieties:** red (most popular), Chioggia (red and white striped flesh), golden, white

**Preparation:** Trim beets with a sharp knife, and peel or scrub with a vegetable brush to wash. Red beets can stain your hands, which will come out with soap and water, but to avoid that, wear gloves when handling.

**Favorite ways to serve:** roasted whole or as fries, pureed into soup, eaten raw and grated into slaws and salads

**Nutritional info:** Beets are rich in fiber, folate, iron, and vitamin C. They also contain nitrates, which are beneficial compounds that may help reduce blood pressure and improve oxygen flow in the body.

**Selection:** Look for beets that are firm to the touch and do not contain any dark bruises or blemishes. If their greens are intact, they should be healthy with strong stems and not wilted.

**Storage:** Beets can last for up to four weeks in a cool, dry place, such as a crisper drawer in the refrigerator. If you purchase beets with their greens, cut them off and use them within a few days.

# Beet Yogurt Dip with Mint

**MAKES ABOUT 2 CUPS / PREP TIME:** 10 minutes

*Earthy beets, tangy full-fat yogurt, and fresh mint prove to be a delectable combination in this unique dip. These three ingredients stand alone, providing enough flavor and variety to keep you coming back to this recipe again and again, which is great, because beet season spans over summer, fall, and winter. Enjoy the dip with pita chips and fresh vegetables in the summer, and serve it on top of warm grain bowls in the colder seasons.*

**1 medium roasted beet, peeled** (see page 42)

**1½ cups full-fat plain Greek yogurt**

**2 tablespoons packed chopped fresh mint leaves, plus more as needed**

**Salt**

1. Using a hand grater, shred the roasted beet into a medium bowl.

2. Add the yogurt and mint. Stir to combine. Taste, and add salt or more mint as needed.

NOTE: To save time if you don't already have a roasted beet on hand, look for pre-roasted options, like Love Beets, that are available at most grocery stores. Store the dip in an airtight container in the refrigerator for up to 5 days. The dip will get more flavorful (and pinker!) the longer you keep it.

# Whole Roasted Beets

**SERVES 4** / **PREP TIME:** 5 minutes / **COOK TIME:** 50 minutes

**4 red beets, trimmed and scrubbed**

**1 tablespoon extra-virgin olive oil**

**Crumbled vegetarian goat cheese, for serving**

**Chopped nuts of your choice, for serving**

1. Preheat the oven to 400°F.

2. Using your hands or a silicone brush, lightly coat each beet with the olive oil.

3. Wrap each beet in a sheet of aluminum foil, and place directly on the center rack of the oven. Bake for 45 to 50 minutes, or until fork-tender. Remove from the oven. Open the foil to let them cool.

4. Under cold running water, remove the skin of each beet with your hands (it should glide right off).

5. Slice the beets, and serve with goat cheese and nuts of your choice.

**NOTE:** You could also serve these drizzled with equal parts melted butter and honey. Store leftovers in an airtight container in the refrigerator for up to 5 days, and use in salads or smoothies.

# Beet Fries with Garlic Tahini

**SERVES 4** / **PREP TIME:** 10 minutes / **COOK TIME:** 30 minutes

*These colorful fries will transform snack time at your house. Roasting beets brings out their natural sweetness, making them a delicious companion to a savory garlic tahini dip. Plus, the deep red color of beets indicates the abundance of betalains, pigments that may act as antioxidants and protect against heart disease and cell damage. These same pigments are also responsible for giving urine a harmless reddish tint after eating beets (so don't panic).*

## FOR THE BEET FRIES

3 medium beets, trimmed,
   peeled, and cut into
   ½-inch-thick strips
1 tablespoon extra-virgin
   olive oil
Salt

## FOR THE GARLIC TAHINI

¼ cup tahini
2 garlic cloves, minced
1 tablespoon apple
   cider vinegar
¼ teaspoon salt

## TO MAKE THE BEET FRIES

1. Preheat the oven to 400°F. Line a baking sheet with parchment paper.

2. On the prepared baking sheet, toss the beets with the olive oil until evenly coated. Season with salt.

3. Transfer the baking sheet to the oven, and roast for 25 to 30 minutes, flipping halfway through, or until the beets are tender. Remove from the oven.

## TO MAKE THE GARLIC TAHINI

4. In a small bowl, whisk together the tahini, garlic, vinegar, and salt. Add water, 1 teaspoon at a time, whisking after each addition, until you reach your desired consistency.

5. Put the beet fries on a serving plate, and serve with the dip in a small bowl on the side.

NOTE: You can use this same method to make fries out of other root vegetables, such as carrots, parsnips, rutabaga, and sweet potatoes.

# Coconut Curry Golden Beet Soup

**SERVES 4** / **PREP TIME:** 10 minutes / **COOK TIME:** 30 minutes

*Thanks to warm spices and velvety coconut milk, this deep yellow soup is the definition of comforting. Enjoy a bowl while you snuggle under a blanket to make it even better. Golden beets are considered by many to be slightly sweeter than their red counterparts, and a combination of curry powder, cumin, ginger, and cinnamon amplifies their sweetness. Top with Paprika-Roasted Chickpeas (page 37) before serving.*

**1 tablespoon extra-virgin olive oil**

**1 sweet onion, diced**

**2 teaspoons curry powder**

**1 teaspoon ground cumin**

**½ teaspoon ground ginger**

**¼ teaspoon ground cinnamon**

**Salt**

**3 medium golden beets, scrubbed, trimmed, and chopped**

**3 cups vegetable broth**

**1 (13½-ounce) can full-fat coconut milk**

1. In a large pot or Dutch oven, warm the olive oil over medium heat.

2. Add the onion, and cook for 3 to 5 minutes, or until tender.

3. Sprinkle in the curry powder, cumin, ginger, and cinnamon. Cook, stirring frequently, for 2 minutes, or until fragrant. Season with salt to taste.

4. Add the beets and vegetable broth.

5. Increase the heat to high, and bring to a boil. Cover, and reduce the heat to medium-low. Cook for about 30 minutes, or until the beets are fork-tender.

6. Add the coconut milk, and stir well. Remove from the heat.

7. Using an immersion blender, puree the soup right in the pot. Spoon into bowls, and enjoy warm.

**NOTE:** I make this recipe with the skins on, but you can peel the beets if you like. You can also use a regular blender for this recipe. To do this safely, fill the blender halfway, and puree the soup in batches. Leave a corner of the lid cracked, or remove the top of the blender and cover it with a folded dish towel to let steam escape as you blend. Be careful not to burn yourself on the hot steam.

# Red Velvet Beet Oatmeal

**SERVES 4** / **PREP TIME:** 5 minutes / **COOK TIME:** 20 minutes

*Who says you can't have dessert for breakfast? Red velvet flavors shine in this healthy spin on a classic sweet treat. Beets and berries provide the red color, while cocoa powder and maple syrup contribute chocolatey sweetness. But instead of experiencing the inevitable sugar crash that comes after eating dessert, you'll be energized and ready to start the day, thanks to steel-cut oats and other high-fiber ingredients.*

**1 cup steel-cut oats**

**1 cup grated raw beets**

**1 tablespoon unsweetened cocoa powder**

**2 to 3 tablespoons maple syrup**

**¼ cup nut butter of your choice**

**2 cups raspberries or strawberries**

1. In a medium saucepan, bring 4 cups of water to a boil over high heat.

2. Add the oats, and cook, stirring frequently, for 3 to 5 minutes, or until thickened.

3. Reduce the heat to low. Cook for 10 to 15 minutes, or until the oats are tender.

4. Add the beets, cocoa powder, maple syrup, and nut butter. Cook for a few minutes, or until the oatmeal has cooked through. Remove from the heat.

5. Transfer the oatmeal to bowls, and serve with the berries.

**NOTE:** You can also use grated roasted beet for this recipe. Cooking time will vary depending on the type of steel-cut oats you use. Use quick-cooking varieties to save time.

# Bok Choy

**Season:** fall, winter

**Flavor profile:** Also known as pak choi, this vegetable is a type of Chinese cabbage that belongs to the same family as broccoli, kale, green cabbage, and turnips. Bok choy has tender green leaves attached to clustered stalks and a white bulbous bottom that's crunchy and juicy. Its mild taste is mellower than cabbage, with hints of celery.

**Pairs with:** soy sauce, garlic, ginger, lemon, miso, hot pepper sauce, apple cider vinegar

**Varieties:** mature (white stalks and dark green leaves), baby (light green or white stalks and green leaves)

**Preparation:** Trim off the base, and wash each leaf well, since dirt can hide in the stalks.

**Favorite ways to serve:** halved and roasted, sautéed, stir-fried

**Nutritional info:** Bok choy is low in calories but very nutrient dense. It is especially rich in the antioxidants vitamin A (carotenoids) and C and provides bone-building calcium.

**Selection:** Choose bok choy that has crisp leaves that are not wilted, browned, or holey. The leaves should be compact, and the stalks should be firm.

**Storage:** Store unwashed in a plastic bag with a few poked holes for up to three days in the refrigerator.

# Sautéed Bok Choy

**SERVES 4** / **PREP TIME:** 5 minutes / **COOK TIME:** 5 to 10 minutes

**1 tablespoon extra-virgin olive oil**

**2 garlic cloves, minced**

**1 teaspoon chopped fresh ginger**

**Pinch red pepper flakes**

**1 bunch bok choy, trimmed and coarsely chopped across the stems**

1. In a skillet, warm the olive oil over medium heat.

2. Add the garlic, ginger, and red pepper flakes. Cook for a few minutes, or until fragrant.

3. Add the bok choy, and cook for 3 to 5 minutes, or until it reaches your desired doneness.

4. To make it more tender, pour in 2 tablespoons of water, cover, and steam for 2 to 3 more minutes. Remove from the heat.

**NOTE:** If you don't have mature bok choy, you can chop up 4 baby bok choy for this recipe.

# Roasted Baby Bok Choy with Spicy Maple Miso

**SERVES 4 / PREP TIME:** 5 minutes / **COOK TIME:** 10 minutes

*Mellow bok choy tastes incredible with a sweet and spicy sauce. The drizzle in this recipe features sweet white miso made from fermented soybeans and grains, which contributes a creamy texture and umami flavor that elevates the entire dish. With only four main ingredients and less than 10 minutes in the oven, it doesn't get much better than this simple vegetable side.*

**FOR THE ROASTED BOK CHOY**

**4 heads baby bok choy, halved lengthwise**
**1 teaspoon extra-virgin olive oil**
**Salt**
**Freshly ground black pepper**

**FOR THE SPICY MAPLE MISO**

**1 tablespoon maple syrup**
**1 tablespoon white miso**
**1 teaspoon sriracha**

**TO MAKE THE ROASTED BOK CHOY**

1. Preheat the oven to 400°F. Line a baking sheet with parchment paper.

2. On the prepared baking sheet, brush the bok choy with the olive oil on both sides. Season with salt and pepper to taste.

3. Arrange the bok choy halves, cut-side up.

4. Transfer the baking sheet to the lowest rack of the oven, and roast for 6 to 8 minutes, flipping halfway through, or until the leaves are wilted and slightly brown. Check frequently to ensure they don't burn. Remove from the oven.

**TO MAKE THE SPICY MAPLE MISO**

5. In a small bowl, mix together the maple syrup, miso, and sriracha.

6. Spoon the mixture over the warm bok choy.

**NOTE:** You can find miso at most large grocery stores in the refrigerated condiment area of the produce section or near the international aisle.

# Broccoli

**Season:** spring, fall, winter

**Flavor profile:** Broccoli resembles a mini tree, with an edible stalk and large head made up of florets. The flavor of broccoli is grassy and earthy and can be slightly bitter when raw. Roasting broccoli makes it sweeter.

**Pairs with:** soy sauce, garlic, ginger, mayonnaise- or yogurt-based sauces, peanuts, red pepper flakes, parmesan and cheddar cheeses, bell peppers, red onion

**Varieties:** belstar, Calabrese, destiny, as well as broccolini (page 55)

**Preparation:** Rinse head under cold running water to clean. Cut off the stalk and pull apart the florets.

**Favorite ways to serve:** roasted, raw in salads, steamed

**Nutritional info:** Broccoli is a member of the cruciferous vegetable family, known for its abundance of health-promoting compounds. One of the compounds, kaempferol, has been shown to fight inflammation and may help protect against chronic diseases. Broccoli is also rich in fiber, vitamin C, and potassium.

**Selection:** Broccoli florets should be tight and green without black or brown spots, and stalks should appear fresh with no browning. Fresh broccoli feels heavy even for its small size.

**Storage:** Keep broccoli unwashed in a loose-fitting plastic bag with some holes to allow air circulation. Store in a produce drawer in the refrigerator for up to one week.

# Garlic-Lemon Roasted Broccoli

**SERVES 4** / **PREP TIME:** 5 minutes / **COOK TIME:** 25 minutes

**1 large head broccoli, cut into florets**

**2 tablespoons extra-virgin olive oil**

**6 garlic cloves, minced**

**2 teaspoons grated lemon zest**

**Salt**

1. Preheat the oven to 400°F. Line a baking sheet with parchment paper.

2. On the prepared baking sheet, using your hands or a spatula, toss the broccoli with the olive oil and garlic until coated.

3. Sprinkle the lemon zest over the broccoli. Season with salt.

4. Transfer the baking sheet to the oven, and bake for 20 to 25 minutes, or until tender and browned. Remove from the oven.

# Honey-Mustard Broccoli and Almond Salad

**SERVES 4 / PREP TIME:** 15 minutes

*Crunchy raw broccoli and almonds pair well in this mayonnaise-free, cold broccoli salad. With a sweet and tangy dressing that's simply irresistible, it will have you coming back for seconds right away. Broccoli salad is a great option for potlucks, holiday parties, and cookouts, and it's highly customizable. Feel free to make ingredient substitutions and additions based on your preferences.*

**FOR THE HONEY-MUSTARD DRESSING**

**¼ cup extra-virgin olive oil**
**2 tablespoons Dijon mustard**
**2 tablespoons honey**
**2 tablespoons apple cider vinegar**

**FOR THE BROCCOLI SALAD**

**8 to 10 cups broccoli florets and chopped stalks (2 to 3 heads)**
**¼ cup chopped red onion**
**½ cup dried cranberries**
**½ cup chopped or slivered almonds**
**Salt**
**Freshly ground black pepper**

**TO MAKE THE HONEY-MUSTARD DRESSING**

1. In a large bowl, mix together the olive oil, mustard, honey, and vinegar.

**TO MAKE THE SALAD**

2. Add the broccoli, onion, dried cranberries, and almonds. Toss until evenly coated. Season with salt and pepper to taste.

**NOTE:** Broccoli salad can keep in an airtight container in the refrigerator for 3 to 5 days. It gets more flavorful the longer it sits. You can add shredded vegetarian cheese or substitute dried cherries for the cranberries and sunflower seeds for the almonds. To make it vegan, use maple syrup instead of honey.

# Cilantro-Lime Riced Broccoli

**MAKES 6 CUPS** / **PREP TIME:** 5 minutes / **COOK TIME:** 5 to 10 minutes

*Move over cauliflower rice, there's a new riced veggie in town! With the flick of a switch, you can make riced broccoli, literally, in seconds. This recipe includes a simple cilantro-lime seasoning that adds Mexican-inspired flavors. You can eat it in place of or in addition to regular rice with bean dishes, burrito bowls, and salads for an added boost of fiber, vitamins, and minerals.*

**1 head broccoli, florets and stalks coarsely chopped**

**1 tablespoon extra-virgin olive oil**

**2 garlic cloves, minced**

**2 scallions, green and white parts, sliced**

**Juice of 1 lime**

**2 tablespoons chopped fresh cilantro**

**Salt**

1. In a food processor, combine the broccoli florets and stalks. Pulse for 30 to 45 seconds, or until they have a rice-like texture.

2. In a large skillet, warm the olive oil over medium heat.

3. Add the garlic, scallions, and broccoli. Cook for 4 to 6 minutes, or until tender and warm. Remove from the heat.

4. Stir in the lime juice and cilantro. Season with salt to taste.

**NOTE:** You can also make riced broccoli by grating it, but this will take longer. Other seasoning ideas include parsley and lemon juice, or turmeric, ginger, and soy sauce.

# Steamed Broccoli with Peanut Sauce

**SERVES 4** / **PREP TIME:** 10 minutes / **COOK TIME:** 10 minutes

*Steaming vegetables is one of the simplest ways to prepare them. It helps maintain their crunch and can even preserve water-soluble nutrients. Steamed broccoli is the perfect side dish for a busy night when you need to put something on the table fast. Whip up the creamy peanut sauce while the broccoli cooks, drizzle it on top of the warm broccoli, and sit back and indulge in this unbelievably easy—and delicious—recipe.*

**FOR THE STEAMED BROCCOLI**

**2 heads broccoli, cut into florets**

**FOR THE PEANUT SAUCE**

**¼ cup creamy peanut butter**

**1 tablespoon freshly squeezed lime juice**

**1 tablespoon rice vinegar**

**1 teaspoon soy sauce**

**½ teaspoon toasted sesame oil**

**1 teaspoon honey**

**1 teaspoon chopped fresh ginger**

**1 garlic clove, minced**

**TO MAKE THE STEAMED BROCCOLI**

1. Fill a large pot with 2 to 3 inches of water. Place a steamer basket inside the pot, and put the broccoli in the basket. Bring to a boil over high heat.

2. Reduce the heat to medium-low. Cover, and cook for 6 to 8 minutes, or until the broccoli is tender but still crisp. Remove from the heat. Transfer to a bowl.

**TO MAKE THE PEANUT SAUCE**

3. In a small bowl, mix together the peanut butter, lime juice, vinegar, soy sauce, sesame oil, honey, ginger, and garlic. Add a few dashes of water as needed until the sauce reaches the desired consistency.

4. Add the sauce to the broccoli, and toss until evenly coated. Serve warm.

**NOTE:** You can also make this recipe without a steamer basket. Just fill the pot with 1 to 2 inches of water, and bring to a boil over high heat. Add the broccoli, cover, and cook for 3 to 4 minutes, or until tender. Drain before serving. To make the dish vegan, use maple syrup in place of honey. You can also use frozen broccoli.

# Classic Broccoli-Cheddar Soup

**SERVES 4 TO 6** / **PREP TIME:** 15 minutes / **COOK TIME:** 15 to 20 minutes

*Broccoli and cheese is an all-star culinary pairing, especially in soup. Whip up this creamy classic with fresh or frozen broccoli florets, cheddar cheese, and other simple ingredients that you likely have on hand. It's warm, flavorful, and easy enough to make on even the busiest nights.*

3 tablespoons
  extra-virgin olive oil or
  unsalted butter
1 yellow onion, diced
2 carrots, sliced
3 garlic cloves, minced
¼ cup all-purpose flour
1 teaspoon salt
½ teaspoon freshly
  ground black pepper
1 teaspoon dry mustard
3 cups vegetable broth
2 cups milk
4 cups broccoli florets
2 cups freshly grated
  vegetarian cheddar
  cheese, plus more
  for serving

1. In a large pot, warm the olive oil over medium heat.

2. Add the onion and carrots. Cook for 3 to 5 minutes, or until tender.

3. Stir in the garlic, and cook for 1 to 2 minutes, or until fragrant.

4. Add the flour, salt, pepper, and dry mustard. Stir until the vegetables are coated.

5. Pour in the broth and milk, stirring well. Bring to a simmer.

6. Add the broccoli and cheddar cheese. Cook for 4 to 5 minutes, or until the cheese has melted and the broccoli is tender. Remove from the heat.

7. Serve the soup warm, garnished with more cheese.

**NOTE:** Frozen broccoli can be used in place of fresh and added to the recipe in the same way. For a richer soup, use half-and-half in place of milk or 2 cups of broth instead of 3. If you prefer pureed soup, blend with an immersion blender before serving.

# Broccolini

**Season:** spring, fall, winter

**Flavor profile:** Broccolini is often referred to as baby broccoli, since that's exactly what it looks like, but it's actually a cross between regular broccoli and Chinese broccoli. It has longer stalks, smaller florets, and a sweeter taste compared to broccoli.

**Pairs with:** soy sauce, garlic, red wine vinegar, oranges and other citrus, Italian herbs and seasonings

**Varieties:** just one (the name "broccolini" is protected under a trademark)

**Preparation:** Rinse the head under cold running water to clean. Trim the ends with a knife.

**Favorite ways to serve:** roasted, lightly blanched

**Nutritional info:** Broccolini has a nutritional profile similar to regular broccoli and other cruciferous vegetables. One cup has more than 15 percent of the Daily Value (DV) for dietary fiber and provides high amounts of vitamins A and C.

**Selection:** Look for broccolini with firm and moist ends that are not dried out, closed heads, and no flowers. Broccolini that has gone bad will have an unpleasant smell and yellowing around the florets.

**Storage:** Store broccolini in a sealed plastic bag in the refrigerator for up to one week. Do not wash or trim until you plan to cook it.

# Roasted Broccolini with Orange Butter

**SERVES 4** / **PREP TIME:** 5 minutes / **COOK TIME:** 15 minutes

2 pounds broccolini
(about 2 bunches),
trimmed

1 tablespoon extra-virgin
olive oil

3 tablespoons
salted butter

2 tablespoons freshly
squeezed orange juice

Pinch red pepper flakes

Grated orange zest,
for serving

1. Preheat the oven to 425°F. Line a baking sheet with parchment paper.

2. On the prepared baking sheet, using your hands, toss the broccolini with the olive oil until evenly coated.

3. Transfer the baking sheet to the oven, and roast for 15 minutes, or until the broccolini is tender and crispy.

4. Meanwhile, in a small saucepan over low heat, combine the butter, orange juice, and red pepper flakes. Keep warm until the broccolini has finished roasting.

5. Remove the broccolini from the oven. Drizzle the butter sauce on top, and sprinkle with orange zest to taste.

# Broccolini Pasta Salad

**SERVES 4** / **PREP TIME:** 10 minutes / **COOK TIME:** 10 minutes

*Broccolini shines in this flavorful pasta salad. With every bite, you'll get hints of this sweet vegetable along with bell pepper, zesty red onion, Italian herbs, and red wine vinegar. Using broccolini instead of large broccoli florets makes the bites more manageable. This main entrée or side dish is simple to prepare, and the recipe makes enough for potlucks and other larger gatherings.*

**FOR THE PASTA SALAD**

8 ounces fusilli pasta

3 cups chopped broccolini, a mix of florets and stalks

1 red bell pepper, seeded and chopped

1 cup halved and sliced red onion

Salt

**FOR THE DRESSING**

½ cup extra-virgin olive oil

¼ cup red wine vinegar

1 tablespoon maple syrup

1 teaspoon dried parsley

½ teaspoon dried basil

¼ teaspoon salt

**TO MAKE THE PASTA SALAD**

1. Bring a large pot of salted water to a boil over high heat.

2. Add the pasta, and cook for 4 to 5 minutes.

3. Add the broccolini, and cook the pasta and broccolini together for 3 minutes, or until the broccolini is slightly tender and the pasta is al dente. Remove from the heat. Drain, and rinse with cold water. Transfer to a large bowl.

4. Add the bell pepper and onion.

**TO MAKE THE DRESSING**

5. In a small bowl, mix together the olive oil, vinegar, maple syrup, parsley, basil, and salt.

6. Add the dressing to the vegetables and pasta, and toss until well combined.

NOTE: This dish tastes even better after sitting for 30 to 60 minutes in the refrigerator. Possible additions include crumbled vegetarian feta cheese, vegetarian mozzarella balls, and fresh herbs instead of dried. You can use Roasted Red Peppers (page 206) instead of raw and substitute penne or rotini pasta if you don't have fusilli.

# Broccoli Rabe

**Season:** spring, fall, winter

**Flavor profile:** Contrary to what its name and appearance suggest, broccoli rabe (or rapini) is not a type of broccoli and is instead related to the turnip. As a result, it has a sharp, bitter flavor. It tastes best when blanched and seasoned with garlic.

**Pairs with:** olive oil, garlic, red pepper flakes, roasted red peppers, pine nuts, parmesan, provolone, smoked cheeses

**Varieties:** just one

**Preparation:** Rinse under cold running water to clean. Trim the ends with a sharp knife.

**Favorite ways to serve:** blanched then sautéed (treat similarly to bitter greens like turnip greens or mustard greens when seasoning)

**Nutritional info:** Broccoli rabe has an impressive nutritional profile, providing high amounts of vitamins A, C, and K. It's also rich in vitamin B5 (pantothenic acid), which aids in extracting energy from proteins, carbohydrates, and fats in the body.

**Selection:** Fresh broccoli rabe has firm stalks and moist ends that are not dried out, with deep green leaves and tightly closed florets. Yellow flowers are a sign that broccoli rabe is past its prime.

**Storage:** Keep broccoli rabe unwashed in a sealed plastic bag in the refrigerator for up to one week.

# Classic Sautéed Broccoli Rabe

**SERVES 4** / **PREP TIME:** 5 minutes / **COOK TIME:** 10 to 15 minutes

1 pound broccoli rabe, trimmed and cut into 2-inch pieces

2 tablespoons extra-virgin olive oil

6 to 8 garlic cloves, minced

Pinch red pepper flakes

Salt

1. Bring a large pot of salted water to a boil over high heat.

2. Add the broccoli rabe and cook for 2 to 3 minutes. Be careful not to overcook, or it will become mushy. Remove from the heat. Drain, rinse with cold water, and pat dry.

3. In a large skillet, warm the olive oil over medium-high heat.

4. Add the garlic and red pepper flakes. Sauté for 1 to 2 minutes, or until fragrant.

5. Add the broccoli rabe and cook for 3 to 6 minutes, or until it reaches your desired doneness. Season with salt to taste. Remove from the heat.

NOTE: Store cooked broccoli rabe in more olive oil and garlic in an airtight container in the refrigerator for up to three days.

# Broccoli Rabe and Provolone Hoagies

**SERVES 4** / **PREP TIME:** 15 minutes / **COOK TIME:** 15 minutes

*Growing up in Philadelphia, I was lucky enough to enjoy broccoli rabe as often as I wanted. I still seek it out at Italian bodegas and restaurants any chance I get when I go back to visit. Although I love garlicky sautéed broccoli rabe on its own, I love it even more when it's nestled between a toasted hoagie roll and melty slices of provolone cheese. Trust me, this simple vegetarian sub is downright delicious.*

**4 (6-inch) Italian or French rolls, halved lengthwise**
**Extra-virgin olive oil, for brushing**
**12 thin vegetarian provolone cheese slices**
**Classic Sautéed Broccoli Rabe** (page 59)

1. Preheat the oven to 400°F. Line a baking sheet with parchment paper.

2. Open the sliced rolls, and arrange them on the prepared baking sheet.

3. Brush the rolls with the olive oil.

4. Transfer the baking sheet to the oven, and bake for 3 to 5 minutes, or until the rolls are slightly toasted. Remove from the oven.

5. Arrange the provolone cheese slices on the cut sides of the tops of each roll, and spread the broccoli rabe evenly on the bottom halves.

6. Return the baking sheet to the oven. Bake for 7 to 10 minutes, rotating halfway through, or until the cheese has melted. Remove from the oven.

7. Carefully replace the roll tops, and use a serrated knife to cut each hoagie in half.

**NOTE:** Though these additions are entirely optional, this sandwich tastes incredible with the Creamy White Bean Dip (page 38) and some Roasted Red Peppers (page 206).

# Brussels Sprouts

**Season:** fall, winter

**Flavor profile:** Raw Brussels sprouts resemble mini cabbages and have a bitter taste and tough texture. When roasted, sautéed, or steamed, Brussels sprouts are more mellow with a slightly nutty aftertaste. Roasting Brussels sprouts brings out their natural sweetness and gives them a deliciously crispy exterior.

**Pairs with:** citrus, balsamic or apple cider vinegar, mustard, sriracha or other hot pepper sauces, honey, maple syrup, apples and apple cider, parmesan and gruyère cheese, miso, walnuts, pine nuts

**Varieties:** green (most common) and purple, resulting from a cross with purple cabbage

**Preparation:** Remove yellow leaves, and use a paring knife to cut off any small areas with holes or damage. Trim the ends, and submerge the sprouts in a bowl of cold water to remove any dirt. Cut in half or use a food processor, mandoline, or knife to shred.

**Favorite ways to serve:** roasted, sautéed, shaved, shredded

**Nutritional info:** Brussels sprouts are rich in fiber, vitamins C and K, and antioxidants. They also have

sulfur-containing compounds known as glucosinolates that break down into isothiocyanates in the body and may exhibit anti-cancer effects.

**Selection:** Brussels sprouts should be firm with compact leaves that are bright green. A few yellow leaves can be normal, but avoid Brussels sprouts with withered leaves that have holes and brown spots. Some stores will sell Brussels sprouts on the stalk as well as loose.

**Storage:** Wait to prepare and wash Brussels sprouts until right before cooking. Store unwashed Brussels sprouts in a plastic bag or airtight container in the crisper drawer of the refrigerator for up to one week. Brussels sprouts on the stalk stay fresh longer, so keep them on the stalk until ready to prepare.

# Crispy Roasted Brussels Sprouts

**SERVES 4** / **PREP TIME:** 10 minutes / **COOK TIME:** 25 minutes

1 pound Brussels sprouts,
    trimmed and halved
2 tablespoons extra-virgin
    olive oil
Salt
Freshly ground
    black pepper

1. Preheat the oven to 450°F. Line a baking sheet with parchment paper.

2. On the prepared baking sheet, toss the Brussels sprouts with the olive oil until coated. Season with salt and pepper.

3. Arrange the Brussels sprouts in an even layer, cut-sides down. Avoid overcrowding to allow room for air to circulate so that they roast and caramelize instead of steaming.

4. Transfer the baking sheet to the oven, and roast for 20 to 25 minutes, or until the Brussels sprouts are crispy on the outside and tender on the inside. Remove from the oven. Season with salt and pepper to taste. Serve warm.

NOTE: For a sweet and spicy variation, toss the sprouts with 1 tablespoon maple syrup and a pinch of red pepper flakes before roasting. You can also sprinkle them with vegetarian parmesan cheese and lemon zest in the last few minutes of cooking.

# Turmeric Riced Brussels Sprouts

**MAKES 4 CUPS** / **PREP TIME:** 10 minutes / **COOK TIME:** 10 minutes

*Bright yellow turmeric rice is a tasty side dish that pairs well with so many main courses. This version features riced Brussels sprouts in place of traditional rice, cooked in coconut oil and anti-inflammatory ground turmeric and ginger for an extra boost of nutrition. It's delicious, colorful, and makes a great base for salads and grain bowls.*

**1 pound Brussels sprouts, trimmed and halved**

**1 tablespoon coconut oil**

**½ teaspoon ground turmeric**

**½ teaspoon onion powder**

**¼ teaspoon ground ginger**

**Salt**

**Freshly ground black pepper**

**¼ cup raisins** (optional)

1. Put the Brussels sprouts in a food processor, and pulse for 30 to 45 seconds, or until they have a rice-like texture. You may need to do this in 2 batches, depending on the size of your food processor.

2. In a large skillet, warm the coconut oil over medium heat.

3. Add the Brussels sprouts, turmeric, onion powder, and ginger. Cook, stirring occasionally, for 5 to 7 minutes, or until tender. Season with salt and pepper to taste. Remove from the heat.

4. Stir in the raisins (if using). Serve warm.

**NOTE:** Substitute frozen riced Brussels sprouts, available at some grocery stores, to save time. You can use 2 tablespoons chopped fresh onion in place of onion powder, if desired.

# Shredded Brussels Sprouts Salad

**SERVES 4 / PREP TIME:** 15 minutes

*Thinly shredded Brussels sprouts are the star ingredient in this easy and delicious salad. With dried cherries, walnuts, and Parmesan cheese, it's sweet, salty, and savory all at the same time. Such a crowd-pleasing flavor profile makes this salad a perfect choice for holiday gatherings, meals with friends, or just a quick weeknight dinner. Add fresh, seasonal fruit like apples or pears for even more fall-inspired flavor.*

## FOR THE SALAD

1 pound Brussels
  sprouts, trimmed
½ cup dried cherries
¼ cup chopped walnuts
¼ cup freshly
  shaved vegetarian
  parmesan cheese

## FOR THE DRESSING

¼ cup extra-virgin olive oil
3 tablespoons apple
  cider vinegar
2 teaspoons maple syrup
1 teaspoon Dijon mustard
Salt
Freshly ground
  black pepper

## TO MAKE THE SALAD

1. Using a mandoline or food processor, shred the Brussels sprouts. If you don't have either, cut the Brussels sprouts in half and then into thin slices using a sharp knife. Put them in a large bowl.

2. Add the dried cherries, walnuts, and parmesan cheese.

## TO MAKE THE DRESSING

3. In a small bowl, whisk together the olive oil, vinegar, maple syrup, and mustard.

4. Add the dressing to the salad, and toss to combine. Season with salt and pepper.

**NOTE:** You can substitute dried cranberries for the cherries. You can also substitute sunflower seeds or pine nuts for the walnuts. Several large grocery chains carry shredded Brussels sprouts in the produce section if you want to save time.

# Skillet Brussels Sprouts Casserole with Pecans

**SERVES 4** / **PREP TIME:** 10 minutes / **COOK TIME:** 20 minutes

*This simple yet decadent recipe has earned major comfort food status. Tender Brussels sprouts are blanketed in a layer of melted gruyère cheese and chopped pecans, making them the ideal side dish for a cold winter's night, Thanksgiving, or Christmas. Though it may be hard to believe that only four main ingredients can provide such a rich flavor, give it a try and you'll see how delicious it is for yourself.*

**1 tablespoon extra-virgin olive oil**

**1 pound Brussels sprouts, trimmed and halved**

**Salt**

**Freshly ground black pepper**

**½ cup heavy cream**

**½ cup freshly grated vegetarian gruyère cheese**

**¼ cup chopped pecans**

1. Preheat the oven to 400°F.

2. In a large oven-safe skillet, warm the olive oil over medium heat.

3. Add the Brussels sprouts, and cook for about 5 minutes, or until slightly softened. Season with salt and pepper to taste. Remove from the heat.

4. Pour in the heavy cream. Sprinkle the gruyère cheese and pecans on top.

5. Transfer the skillet to the oven, and bake for 12 to 15 minutes, or until the cheese is bubbling and melted and the Brussels sprouts are tender. Remove from the oven. Serve warm.

**NOTE:** Possible additions include a diced shallot or diced apple sautéed with the Brussels sprouts and a pinch of cinnamon.

# Brussels Sprouts al Pastor Tacos

**MAKES 6 TACOS / PREP TIME:** 10 minutes / **COOK TIME:** 15 minutes

*Al pastor tacos are usually made with pork that has been marinated in a sauce consisting of pineapple, vinegar, and spices. In this vegetarian version, shredded Brussels sprouts are cooked in a homemade al pastor sauce before being nestled into warm tortillas and topped with salty cotija cheese and fresh cilantro. Even though the Brussels sprouts in this recipe aren't roasted on a spit like al pastor pork, they're still sweet, spicy, and downright delicious.*

1 tablespoon extra-virgin olive oil

1 pound Brussels sprouts, trimmed and shredded or thinly sliced

½ cup chopped red onion

3 garlic cloves, minced

2 canned chipotle peppers in adobo sauce, plus 1 tablespoon sauce

¼ cup white vinegar

1 teaspoon dried oregano

1 teaspoon smoked paprika

3 cups chopped pineapple, divided

6 corn or flour tortillas, warmed

1 cup crumbled cotija cheese (see note)

Chopped fresh cilantro, for serving

1. In a large skillet, warm the olive oil over medium heat.

2. Add the Brussels sprouts and onion. Cook for 5 to 7 minutes, or until the Brussels sprouts have softened.

3. Meanwhile, to make the sauce, in a blender, combine the garlic, chipotle peppers and adobo sauce, vinegar, oregano, paprika, and 1 cup of pineapple. Blend until smooth.

4. Pour the sauce into the skillet, and stir well to ensure that the Brussels sprouts are evenly coated. Cook for another 3 to 5 minutes, or until warmed through. Remove from the heat.

5. Spoon the Brussels sprouts into the tortillas.

6. Divide the remaining 2 cups of pineapple equally among the tacos, and top with the cotija cheese and cilantro.

NOTE: Cotija cheese is typically made with animal rennet. If this is a concern, as an alternative, you can use vegetarian parmesan cheese, which is made with microbial or vegetarian rennet. To warm the tortillas, heat in a separate skillet for about 1 minute on each side. You can also wrap the stack of tortillas in aluminum foil and heat them on the center rack of the oven for 10 minutes at 350°F.

# Cabbage

**Season:** spring, fall, winter

**Flavor profile:** Though raw cabbage has a bitter taste and a tough, rubbery texture, cooked cabbage is sweeter and milder with a buttery mouthfeel. Due to these differences, raw cabbage tastes best when it is thinly sliced and tossed with a hearty dressing. Cooked cabbage is more tender and can be enjoyed as large wedges or smaller pieces.

**Pairs with:** vinegar, lime juice, peanut sauce, soy sauce, butter, celery salt, garlic, black pepper, red pepper flakes, yogurt, apples, pineapple, onions, potatoes

**Varieties:** green, red (or purple), napa (green, oval-shaped), Savoy (dark green, crinkly leaves)

**Preparation:** Remove the outer leaves, cut in half, and wash under cold, running water. Cut into quarters, then cut off the core at the bottom of each wedge before cooking or shredding into smaller pieces with a knife or mandoline.

**Favorite ways to serve:** raw in salads and slaws, roasted, braised

**Nutritional info:** All cabbage varieties are low in calories, high in fiber, and rich in vitamins C and K. Red cabbage gets its color from pigments known as anthocyanins that may help decrease blood pressure and fight inflammation in the body associated with heart disease.

**Selection:** Choose heads of cabbage that feel heavy, with tightly packed leaves and firm stems. Wilted or discolored leaves are a sign that the cabbage is old or was mishandled.

**Storage:** Whole heads of cabbage can be stored in a plastic bag in the crisper drawer of the refrigerator for up to two weeks. Cabbage halves or quarters that have already been cut should be wrapped tightly in plastic wrap before being stored.

# Roasted Cabbage Wedges

**SERVES 4** / **PREP TIME:** 5 minutes / **COOK TIME:** 30 minutes

1 head cabbage,
   cut into 8 wedges
2 tablespoons extra-virgin
   olive oil
Salt
Freshly ground
   black pepper
4 lemon wedges,
   for serving (optional)

1.  Preheat the oven to 400°F. Line a baking sheet with parchment paper.

2.  Arrange the cabbage wedges in a single layer on the prepared baking sheet.

3.  Brush each side of the wedges with the olive oil. Season with salt and pepper.

4.  Transfer the baking sheet to the oven, and roast for 25 to 30 minutes, flipping halfway through, or until the cabbage is browned and tender. Remove from the oven.

5.  Serve warm with a squeeze of lemon juice (if using).

# Braised Cabbage, Apples, and White Beans

**SERVES 4** / **PREP TIME:** 10 minutes / **COOK TIME:** 20 minutes

*Braised cabbage shines in this hearty vegetarian main dish. Fresh apples and apple cider vinegar offer a sweet, tangy taste that beautifully complements the buttery cabbage and creamy white beans. The delicious combination of textures and flavors in this one-pan recipe, coupled with the short prep and cook time, make it a go-to dish for weeknight meals. Plus, you can use any variety of cabbage.*

**2 tablespoons unsalted butter**

**1 small head cabbage, shredded**

**2 Pink Lady apples, diced**

**¼ cup apple cider vinegar**

**½ teaspoon salt, plus more as needed**

**1 (15-ounce) can cannellini beans, drained and rinsed**

1. In a large skillet, melt the butter over medium heat.

2. Add the cabbage, and cook for 3 to 5 minutes, or until slightly tender.

3. Add the apples, and cook for 3 to 4 minutes, or until softened.

4. Add the vinegar, ¼ cup of water, and the salt.

5. Reduce the heat to low. Cover, and cook for 5 to 7 minutes, or until the cabbage is buttery and the apples are tender.

6. Remove the cover, stir in the beans, and cook for 3 to 4 minutes, or until warmed through. Remove from the heat. Serve warm.

**NOTE:** Substitute chickpeas or navy beans for the cannellini, if desired. You can also use different types of apples. Store leftovers in an airtight container in the refrigerator for up to 4 days.

# Quick Sesame-Soy Red Cabbage Slaw

**SERVES 6 / PREP TIME:** 20 minutes

*Brighten up your plate with this colorful slaw coated in a sesame-soy dressing. With fresh cilantro, ginger, and scallions, each bite packs a ton of flavor. Bring this slaw to your next potluck, serve it alongside a stir-fry, use it as a taco topping, or bulk it up with edamame or tofu to make it a main dish. Extra vegetables that you have on hand, like bell peppers or cucumbers, are totally fair game to add.*

**FOR THE DRESSING**

- 2 tablespoons extra-virgin olive oil
- 1 tablespoon toasted sesame oil
- 3 tablespoons rice vinegar
- 1 tablespoon soy sauce
- 2 teaspoons finely chopped fresh ginger
- 1 tablespoon honey

**FOR THE SLAW**

- 1 small head red cabbage, shredded
- 3 scallions, green and white parts, thinly sliced
- 1 cup shredded carrots
- ¼ cup chopped fresh cilantro

**TO MAKE THE DRESSING**

1. In a large bowl, whisk together the olive oil, sesame oil, vinegar, soy sauce, ginger, and honey.

**TO MAKE THE SLAW**

2. Add the cabbage, scallions, carrots, and cilantro. Toss until evenly coated. Serve right away, or cover with plastic wrap and store in the refrigerator until ready to serve.

NOTE: Possible additions include 2 tablespoons chopped fresh mint or basil, chopped peanuts, or sesame seeds. This slaw can be stored in an airtight container in the refrigerator for up to 3 days. Stir well before serving.

# Cabbage and Pineapple Salad with Greek Yogurt Dressing

**SERVES 6 / PREP TIME:** 15 minutes, plus 1 hour to chill

*This flavorful recipe is a unique, sweet twist on coleslaw. Pineapple, lime juice, and creamy Greek yogurt make it the ultimate warm weather dish. Be sure to let it sit in the refrigerator for an hour or two before serving, so that the cabbage gets tender and the flavors meld together. This extra step will ensure that it's a hit at summer potlucks and cookouts.*

### FOR THE SALAD

1 small head green cabbage, shredded
1 (20-ounce) can pineapple chunks with their juice

### FOR THE DRESSING

¼ cup full-fat plain Greek yogurt
1 tablespoon honey
1 tablespoon freshly squeezed lime juice
Salt

### TO MAKE THE SALAD

1. Put the cabbage in a large mixing bowl.
2. Using a slotted spoon, scoop the pineapple tidbits out of the can, add them to the cabbage, and stir to combine. Reserve 3 tablespoons of the juice for the dressing.

### TO MAKE THE DRESSING

3. In a separate bowl, mix together the yogurt, reserved pineapple juice, honey, and lime juice.
4. Add the dressing to the salad, and toss until evenly coated. Season with salt to taste. Cover with plastic wrap, and refrigerate for at least 1 hour before serving.

NOTE: Use bagged coleslaw mix instead of freshly shredded cabbage to save time. Store leftovers in an airtight container in the refrigerator for up to 3 days.

# Carrots

**Season:** spring, summer, fall, winter

**Flavor profile:** One of the most universally loved vegetables, carrots have a sweet but slightly earthy flavor and crunchy texture. Cooking carrots makes them tender and sweeter, but overdoing it can make them mushy. The pleasing taste of carrots lends itself to a wide range of dishes.

**Pairs with:** savory herbs like rosemary, thyme, and dill, as well as cinnamon, nutmeg, cardamom, soy sauce, ginger, tahini, dates, maple syrup, honey, celery, onions

**Varieties:** orange, purple, yellow, white

**Preparation:** Remove the leaves if attached, and trim the ends. Use a vegetable brush to scrub them clean or a swivel peeler to remove the skin. Keep whole, cut with a knife, or shred with a hand grater.

**Favorite ways to serve:** raw, roasted, blended into soups and dressings

**Nutritional info:** Carrots are well-known for being high in beta-carotene, the pigment that gives them their orange

color. In the body, beta-carotene gets converted into the antioxidant vitamin A, which is vital to good eyesight, skin health, and brain function.

**Selection:** Fresh carrots are bright in color and have firm skin that's free of splitting or cracks. If the leaves are attached, they should be vibrant and not wilted.

**Storage:** Store carrots in an unsealed plastic bag in the refrigerator for at least two weeks or sometimes longer. Remove any greens before storing, but do not clean, trim, or cut the carrots until ready to cook.

# Cardamom-Maple Roasted Baby Carrots

**SERVES 4** / **PREP TIME:** 5 minutes / **COOK TIME:** 30 minutes

1 pound baby carrots

2 tablespoons extra-virgin olive oil

2 tablespoons maple syrup

¾ teaspoon ground cardamom

Salt

1. Preheat the oven to 400°F. Line a baking sheet with parchment paper.

2. Put the carrots on the prepared baking sheet.

3. In a small bowl, whisk together the olive oil, maple syrup, and cardamom.

4. Drizzle the mixture over the carrots. Using your hands or a rubber spatula, toss until evenly coated. Season with salt.

5. Arrange the carrots in a single layer.

6. Transfer the baking sheet to the oven, and bake for 25 to 30 minutes, or until the carrots are fork-tender. Remove from the oven. Serve hot.

# Carrot Soup with Rosemary-Thyme Pecans

**SERVES 4** / **PREP TIME:** 15 minutes / **COOK TIME:** 30 to 35 minutes

*Basic carrot soup gets an upgrade from the addition of herbed pecans cooked in butter and brown sugar. The flavorful, crunchy topping brings out the similarly sweet and earthy flavor of carrots. Serve this soup for lunch, dinner, or a holiday meal. If you don't own an immersion blender, see page 27 for notes on making this in a regular blender.*

**FOR THE ROSEMARY-THYME PECANS**

2 tablespoons
  unsalted butter
1 cup chopped pecans
1 tablespoon fresh
  thyme leaves
1 tablespoon chopped
  fresh rosemary
1 teaspoon light
  brown sugar

**FOR THE SOUP**

2 tablespoons extra-virgin
  olive oil
1 sweet onion, diced
3 garlic cloves, minced
8 large carrots, sliced
4 cups vegetable broth
Salt
Freshly ground
  black pepper

**TO MAKE THE ROSEMARY-THYME PECANS**

1. In a small skillet, melt the butter over medium heat.

2. Add the pecans, thyme, rosemary, and sugar. Cook, stirring frequently to avoid burning, for 4 to 5 minutes, or until the pecans are fragrant. Remove from the heat.

**TO MAKE THE SOUP**

3. In a large soup pot or Dutch oven, warm the olive oil over medium-high heat.

4. Add the onion, garlic, and carrots. Cook for 5 to 7 minutes, or until slightly tender.

5. Pour in the broth, and bring to a boil.

6. Reduce the heat to medium-low. Cover, and cook for about 20 minutes, or until the carrots are tender. Season with salt and pepper. Remove from the heat.

7. Using an immersion blender, puree the soup in the pot, or transfer it in batches to a regular blender and puree.

8. Serve the soup in bowls, and top with a sprinkling of the pecans.

# Matchstick Carrot and Edamame Salad

**SERVES 4 / PREP TIME:** 10 minutes

*Cutting carrots into matchsticks is a fun and visually appealing way to prepare this versatile vegetable. Only three main ingredients make up the base of this salad, and the delicious lime-infused sesame dressing comes together with basic pantry ingredients. The addition of protein-packed edamame promotes this recipe from side to main dish. For an even prettier dish, use multicolored carrots.*

**FOR THE DRESSING**

1 tablespoon toasted
  sesame oil
1 tablespoon rice vinegar
Juice of 1 lime
2 teaspoons honey
2 garlic cloves, minced

**FOR THE SALAD**

3 carrots, cut
  into matchsticks
2 scallions, green and
  white parts, thinly sliced
1 cup cooked edamame

**TO MAKE THE DRESSING**

1. In a medium bowl, whisk together the sesame oil, vinegar, lime juice, honey, and garlic.

**TO MAKE THE SALAD**

2. Add the carrots, scallions, and edamame. Toss until evenly coated. Serve immediately.

**NOTE:** Store leftovers in an airtight container in the refrigerator for up to 3 days. Feel free to add sesame seeds for additional flavor.

# Roasted Carrot and Tahini Dressing

**MAKES ABOUT 1 CUP** / **PREP TIME:** 10 minutes / **COOK TIME:** 30 minutes

*Carrots are the go-to veggie to pair with dips and dressings, but they can also shine as the star ingredient of condiments. Loosely inspired by the carrot dressing sold at Trader Joe's, this tahini-based recipe is made with sweet roasted carrots and zesty ginger. It has a fibrous texture and phenomenal taste and makes for a great addition to grain bowls and roasted vegetables like cabbage, bok choy, and broccoli.*

**2 cups sliced carrots**

**2 tablespoons extra-virgin olive oil, divided**

**1 tablespoon chopped fresh ginger**

**1 tablespoon maple syrup**

**1 tablespoon soy sauce**

**¼ cup tahini**

1. Preheat the oven to 400°F. Line a baking sheet with parchment paper.

2. Arrange the carrots in a single layer on the prepared baking sheet.

3. Drizzle the carrots with 1 tablespoon of olive oil.

4. Transfer the baking sheet to the oven, and bake for 25 to 30 minutes, or until the carrots are tender. Remove from the oven.

5. In a blender, combine the carrots, remaining 1 tablespoon of olive oil, the ginger, maple syrup, soy sauce, and tahini. Blend, adding water 1 tablespoon at a time and using a spatula to scrape down the sides of the blender to reach the desired consistency, or until smooth.

**NOTE:** Store in a glass jar in the refrigerator for up to one week.

# Salt and Vinegar Carrot Crisps

**MAKES ABOUT 1 CUP / PREP TIME:** 40 minutes / **COOK TIME:** 20 to 25 minutes

*If you're a fan of salt and vinegar chips, you will love this vegetable-forward twist on that iconic flavor profile. After being soaked in apple cider vinegar and baked in the oven, thinly sliced carrots shrivel into small crisps that pack a ton of flavor for their size. Enjoy them on top of salads, soups, and popcorn or mixed into savory trail mixes.*

**2 carrots**
**¾ cup apple cider vinegar**
**Nonstick cooking spray**
**Salt**

1. Using a mandoline or a swivel peeler, thinly slice or shave the carrots.

2. In a bowl, submerge the carrots in the vinegar, and let sit for 25 to 30 minutes.

3. Preheat the oven to 400°F. Lightly coat 2 baking sheets with cooking spray.

4. Using a slotted spoon or tongs, remove the carrot slices from the vinegar, place onto paper towels, and pat dry.

5. Arrange the carrots in a single layer on each baking sheet. Season liberally with salt.

6. Transfer the baking sheets to the oven, and bake for 10 to 15 minutes. Remove any carrots that are already crispy and put them on a plate to cool. Continue to bake for another 5 to 10 minutes, or until the rest of the carrots are crispy. Watch them closely, and remove pieces as they get crispy to avoid burning. Let the crisps cool at room temperature before seasoning with more salt to taste.

**NOTE:** These crisps taste best when consumed within a couple days, since they start to lose their crispiness over time. Store them in a jar at room temperature.

# No-Bake Carrot Cake Bites

**MAKES 12 BITES** / **PREP TIME:** 15 minutes, plus 30 minutes to 1 hour to chill

*Carrot cake is arguably one of the best ways to eat carrots, and these bite-size treats make it easy to enjoy the delicious flavors of this dessert at any time of day. Made with shredded carrots, pecans, chia seeds, and medjool dates, they're full of fiber and healthy fats to keep you energized and satisfied. Enjoy one or two with your breakfast, or serve them as dessert.*

**¾ cup finely shredded carrots (about 2 carrots)**

**1 cup pecans**

**12 pitted medjool dates**

**1 tablespoon chia seeds**

**1 teaspoon ground cinnamon**

**1 teaspoon vanilla extract**

**¼ teaspoon ground ginger**

**¼ teaspoon salt**

1. In a food processor, combine the carrots, pecans, dates, chia seeds, cinnamon, vanilla, ginger, and salt. Pulse until well combined, stopping to scrape down the sides with a rubber spatula as needed.

2. Roll the mixture into 12 balls, and put them on a plate. Cover with plastic wrap, and refrigerate for 30 minutes to 1 hour, or until firm.

**NOTE:** To ensure that your carrots are finely shredded, use a food processor or hand grater to prepare them. Store these bites in an airtight container in the refrigerator for up to 1 week.

# Cauliflower and Romanesco

**Season:** fall, winter

**Flavor profile:** Cauliflower looks similar to broccoli but with white and more densely packed florets. It has a delicate flavor that's often considered nuttier and sweeter than broccoli and can easily soak up other seasonings.

**Pairs with:** lemon, lime, salt, black pepper, most fresh herbs, capers, honey, curry, red pepper flakes, hot sauces, garlic, tahini, peanut butter

**Varieties:** white, orange, purple, romanesco (a green variety with cone-shaped florets that have a mesmerizing spiral pattern; sometimes referred to as a type of broccoli)

**Preparation:** Remove the leaves, and cut off the bottom stem. Rinse well upside down under cold running water to clean. Cut into quarters, and using your hands or a knife, break up the florets.

**Favorite ways to serve:** processed into rice, roasted, combined with hearty, flavorful dressings

**Nutritional info:** Although it contains a variety of nutrients, cauliflower is an especially good source of vitamins C and K. This vegetable also provides choline, a compound that's important for a healthy brain and nervous system.

**Selection:** Because of the white florets, it's easy to spot cauliflower that has discoloration. Look for heads that are bright white with firm stems and no brown or black spots.

**Storage:** Whole heads of cauliflower can last in a perforated plastic bag in the produce drawer in the refrigerator for up to one week. Florets that have already been cut up should be stored in an airtight container.

# Turmeric Cauliflower Steaks

**SERVES 4** / **PREP TIME:** 5 minutes / **COOK TIME:** 30 minutes

1 head cauliflower

1 tablespoon extra-virgin
  olive oil

1 teaspoon
  ground turmeric

½ teaspoon garlic powder

Salt

Freshly ground
  black pepper

1. Preheat the oven to 400°F. Line a baking sheet with parchment paper.

2. Cut the cauliflower into 1½-inch-thick slices lengthwise from the head through the core. Depending on the size of the cauliflower, you will get 4 to 6 flat pieces that resemble steaks.

3. In a small bowl, mix together the olive oil, turmeric, and garlic powder.

4. On the prepared baking sheet, brush the mixture onto both sides of the cauliflower steaks. Season with salt and pepper.

5. Arrange the steaks in a single layer.

6. Transfer the baking sheet to the oven, and bake for 25 to 30 minutes, flipping halfway through, or until the cauliflower is tender and browned. Remove from the oven.

# Buffalo Cauliflower Wings with Greek Yogurt Ranch

**SERVES 4** / **PREP TIME:** 10 minutes / **COOK TIME:** 40 minutes

*The shape of cauliflower florets makes it easy to turn them into vegetable-based substitutions for chicken wings, and cauliflower can easily soak up the flavors of a delicious sauce. My spin on cauliflower "wings" features spicy Buffalo sauce and a cooling yogurt-based ranch. It will be hard to resist the temptation to lick your fingers with this one.*

**FOR THE GREEK YOGURT RANCH**

½ cup plain Greek yogurt
1 teaspoon garlic powder
½ teaspoon dried dill
½ teaspoon onion powder

**FOR THE CAULIFLOWER WINGS**

½ cup all-purpose flour
2 teaspoons garlic powder
¼ teaspoon salt
½ cup milk of your choice
1 head cauliflower, cut into florets
¾ cup Buffalo sauce
1 tablespoon unsalted butter, melted

**TO MAKE THE GREEK YOGURT RANCH**

1. In a small bowl, mix together the yogurt, garlic powder, dill, and onion powder.

2. Add water to thin, 1 teaspoon at a time, as needed.

**TO MAKE THE CAULIFLOWER WINGS**

3. Preheat the oven to 450°F. Line a baking sheet with parchment paper.

4. In a bowl, whisk together the flour, garlic powder, salt, and milk.

5. Add the cauliflower, and toss until well coated.

6. Arrange the cauliflower in an even layer on the prepared baking sheet.

7. Transfer the baking sheet to the oven, and roast for 20 to 25 minutes, flipping halfway through, or until the cauliflower is softened. Remove from the oven.

8. In a small bowl, whisk together the Buffalo sauce and butter.

9. Pour the mixture over the cauliflower, and toss until well coated.

10. Return the baking sheet to the oven, and roast for 15 minutes, or until the cauliflower is tender and slightly browned. Remove from the oven.

11. Put the cauliflower wings in a serving dish, and serve with the ranch on the side.

NOTE: You can also use barbecue sauce in place of Buffalo sauce for this recipe.

# Spiced Cauliflower, Chickpea, and Raisin Salad

**SERVES 4 / PREP TIME:** 10 minutes / **COOK TIME:** 30 minutes

*This seemingly simple roasted cauliflower main dish has a complex flavor profile, thanks to cumin, cinnamon, and a lemon-honey dressing. The chickpeas and raisins add two more textures that round out the whole recipe. It's a good option to prep in advance and bring to work or school for lunch, especially since it can be served warm or cold.*

## FOR THE SALAD

- 1 tablespoon extra-virgin olive oil
- ½ teaspoon ground cinnamon
- ½ teaspoon ground cumin
- ¼ teaspoon salt
- 1 head cauliflower, cut into florets
- ¼ cup raisins
- 1 (15-ounce) can chickpeas, drained and rinsed

## FOR THE DRESSING

- 3 tablespoons extra-virgin olive oil
- Juice of 1 lemon
- 2 teaspoons honey
- 1 teaspoon Dijon mustard

## TO MAKE THE SALAD

1. Preheat the oven to 400°F. Line a baking sheet with parchment paper.
2. In a large bowl, whisk together the olive oil, cinnamon, cumin, and salt.
3. Add the cauliflower, and toss until evenly coated.
4. Arrange the cauliflower in an even layer on the baking sheet.
5. Transfer the baking sheet to the oven and bake for 25 to 30 minutes, or until the cauliflower is tender. Remove from the oven. Return to the same bowl.
6. Add the raisins and chickpeas and toss.

## TO MAKE THE DRESSING

7. In a small bowl, mix together the olive oil, lemon juice, honey, and mustard.
8. Add the dressing to the cauliflower, and toss until evenly coated.

**NOTE:** Possible additions include chopped fresh herbs like mint or cilantro, slivered almonds, and crumbled vegetarian goat or feta cheese.

# Riced Cauliflower Burrito Bowls

**SERVES 4** / **PREP TIME:** 15 minutes / **COOK TIME:** 10 minutes

*Cauliflower can be credited as the original "riced" vegetable, and it's no wonder why it became so popular. Making cauliflower rice is incredibly easy and makes eating more vegetables even easier. Not to mention you can find premade cauliflower rice at most stores, both fresh and frozen, which can help you cut back on prep time for this recipe. Beans, avocado, salsa, and your other favorite burrito fixings turn this into a filling meal.*

**1 head cauliflower, cut into florets**
**1 tablespoon extra-virgin olive oil**
**2 garlic cloves, minced**
**Salt**
**Freshly ground black pepper**
**1 (15-ounce) can black beans, drained and rinsed**
**Avocado-Lime Mash** (page 29)
**1 cup Arugula Salsa Verde** (page 18) **or salsa of choice**
**1 cup shredded vegetarian Mexican cheese**
**Lime wedges, for serving**

1. Put the cauliflower in a food processor, and pulse until it has a rice-like texture. Do this in batches if you have a small food processor.

2. In a skillet, warm the olive oil over medium heat.

3. Add the cauliflower and garlic. Cook for 5 to 7 minutes, or until tender. Season with salt and pepper to taste. Remove from the heat. Divide evenly between 2 bowls.

4. Top each bowl with equal amounts of beans, avocado mash, salsa, and cheese. Mix together before eating.

5. Serve the bowls with lime wedges.

**NOTE:** This recipe can be prepped in advance for easy lunches and dinners throughout the week, but keep in mind that you may want to make the avocado mash right before serving so that it doesn't brown. Store in airtight containers in the refrigerator for up to four days.

# Roasted Romanesco

**SERVES 4 / PREP TIME:** 5 minutes / **COOK TIME:** 25 minutes

*Several years ago, romanesco was one of the first vegetables I received in my CSA share. I was mesmerized by its beautiful green florets and their intricate pattern, and once I tasted it, I knew I would be a fan for life. Romanesco is crunchier and even more delicious than other types of cauliflower, especially when roasted with basic ingredients. If this is your first time experimenting with this vegetable, you're in for a real treat.*

**1 head romanesco, cut into florets**

**1 to 2 tablespoons extra-virgin olive oil**

**Salt**

**Freshly ground black pepper**

1. Preheat the oven to 425°F. Line a baking sheet with aluminum foil.

2. On the prepared baking sheet, using your hands or a rubber spatula, toss the romanesco with the olive oil (enough to lightly coat). Season generously with salt and pepper.

3. Arrange the romanesco in a single layer.

4. Transfer the baking sheet to the oven, and roast for 20 to 25 minutes, or until the romanesco is tender and browned. Remove from the oven.

# Greek Romanesco and Orzo Salad

**SERVES 4 / PREP TIME:** 10 minutes

*Not every recipe can be fresh, flavorful, and beautiful at the same time, but this romanesco pasta salad checks all of those boxes. It's flavored with Greek-inspired ingredients, like capers, parsley, and lemon juice, and finished with salty feta. If this dish jumps out at you as a must-make (and believe me, it is), you can track down romanesco at farmers' markets and most local food co-ops, or you may receive it in a CSA share.*

### FOR THE DRESSING

¼ cup extra-virgin olive oil
2 tablespoons capers
1 garlic clove, minced
Juice of ½ lemon

### FOR THE SALAD

**Roasted Romanesco**
  (page 86)
2 cups cooked orzo pasta
½ cup crumbled
  vegetarian feta cheese
2 tablespoons chopped
  fresh parsley
Sea salt
Freshly ground
  black pepper

**TO MAKE THE SALAD**

1. In a large bowl, whisk together the olive oil, capers, garlic, and lemon juice.

**TO MAKE THE DRESSING**

2. Add the romanesco, pasta, feta cheese, and parsley. Season with salt and pepper to taste. Toss until coated evenly.

**NOTE:** This salad stores well in the refrigerator in an air-tight container for up to 5 days. Add a squeeze of lemon juice to freshen it up before serving.

# Celery

**Season:** spring, summer, fall

**Flavor profile:** Known for its distinct, stringy texture, celery has an earthy, mineral-like taste. To some, celery has a salty aftertaste, as a result of its relatively higher natural sodium content compared to other vegetables.

**Pairs with:** citrus, nut butters, dried fruits, Buffalo sauce, hot sauce, cream, mayonnaise, yogurt, blue cheese, carrots, onions

**Varieties:** celery (thicker stalks), leaf celery (thinner stalks, with aromatic leaves)

**Preparation:** Separate each stalk from the bunch, and trim off the bottoms and tops. Wash the stalks under cold running water, using your hands to rub off any dirt. Use a sharp knife to cut the stalks into pieces of your desired size. Remove and discard any leaves, or keep them to add to dishes as garnish.

**Favorite ways to serve:** raw and stuffed, cooked in sauces and soups

**Nutritional info:** Celery is well-known for being low in calories and mostly made of water. However, it also provides fiber, antioxidants, and a compound called apiuman that may help strengthen the stomach lining and prevent stomach ulcers.

**Selection:** Look for firm stalks and light green leaves, and avoid celery that appears wilted, soggy, or dried out. It should feel crisp and not rubbery to the touch.

**Storage:** Wrapping celery in aluminum foil helps prevent moisture from leaking out and will keep it from getting mushy and limp. Store it in the produce drawer in the refrigerator for up to one week. Celery that has already been cut should be submerged in water in an airtight container and refrigerated.

# Celery with Almond Butter and Pomegranate

**SERVES 4 / PREP TIME:** 5 minutes

**8 celery stalks, cut into 3-inch-long pieces**

**¼ cup almond butter**

**2 tablespoons pomegranate arils**

**Ground cinnamon**

1. Using a butter knife or spoon, stuff each celery piece with the almond butter.

2. Press the pomegranate arils into the almond butter, sprinkle with cinnamon, and serve.

# Celery, Apple, and Blue Cheese Salad

**SERVES 4 / PREP TIME:** 15 minutes

*Celery and blue cheese are no doubt a winning pair, but they're usually served as condiments to counteract spicy flavors (such as with Buffalo wings). This simple salad proves that they have a place together at the table in a different way. Apple and pistachios boost the crunch factor, while the tangy mustard dressing makes it hard to resist a second helping. Once you try this recipe, you'll see celery as the all-star ingredient it truly is.*

**6 celery stalks,**
  **thinly sliced**
**1 Granny Smith apple,**
  **thinly sliced**
**¼ cup crumbled**
  **blue cheese**
**¼ cup shelled pistachios**
**Shallot-Dijon Vinaigrette**
  (page 233)

1. In a medium bowl, mix together the celery, apple, blue cheese, and pistachios.

2. Add the vinaigrette, and toss until evenly coated.

**NOTE:** You can make this dish in advance, but wait to add the dressing until right before serving. Store leftovers in an airtight container in the refrigerator for up to 3 days.

# Creamy Celery Sauce

**MAKES ABOUT 2 CUPS** / **PREP TIME:** 10 minutes / **COOK TIME:** 20 minutes

*Inspired by cream of celery soup, this recipe showcases the incredible flavor of cooked celery. Small pieces of this earthy vegetable, perfectly complemented by sweet shallot, garlic, and fresh thyme, are present in every bite. I highly recommend tossing cooked pasta in this rich sauce for a comforting meal.*

**2 tablespoons unsalted butter**

**5 celery stalks, finely chopped**

**1 shallot, diced**

**3 garlic cloves, minced**

**1 tablespoon fresh thyme leaves**

**2 tablespoons all-purpose flour**

**1 cup milk**

**Salt**

**Freshly ground black pepper**

**Cooked pasta, for serving**

1. In a large skillet, melt the butter over medium heat.

2. Add the celery, shallot, and garlic. Cook for 5 to 7 minutes, or until tender.

3. Add the thyme and flour. Stir until the vegetables are coated.

4. Pour in the milk.

5. Reduce the heat to medium-low. Simmer, stirring frequently, for 5 to 8 minutes, or until the sauce thickens. Season with salt and pepper to taste. Remove from the heat.

6. Add the cooked pasta, and toss until well coated.

**NOTE:** Serve with red pepper flakes, chopped fresh parsley, and lemon juice for added flavor. You can also use this sauce on top of cauliflower or kohlrabi steaks or toss it with vegetable "noodles."

# Celery Root

**Favorite ways to serve:** roasted, mashed, blended into soups

**Nutritional info:** Celery root is loaded with vitamins and minerals but low in carbohydrates, making it a good alternative to potatoes for those watching their carb intake. It's particularly rich in fat-soluble vitamin K and thus may support healthy blood clotting.

**Selection:** To choose fresh celery root, make sure it is firm to the touch with brown skin. It's normal to see a few hints of green around the top of the vegetable where the stalks were removed, but this should not be widespread. If the stalks are still attached, make sure they are firm and have fresh leaves.

**Storage:** Keep in a perforated plastic bag in the produce drawer in the refrigerator for up to two weeks.

**Season:** fall, winter

**Flavor profile:** Celery root, also known as celeriac, is a knobby root vegetable with potato-like, white flesh and brown skin that's studded with bumps and ridges. As a relative of classic celery, it has a similar taste that's milder with nutty undertones.

**Pairs with:** butter, cream, apples, lemon, garlic, onion, potatoes, honey, mustard

**Varieties:** just one

**Preparation:** Trim the ends, and use a swivel peeler to remove the skin. For skin stuck in the ridges, use a paring knife to make small cuts to remove it. Dice before roasting, boiling, or sautéing.

# Roasted Celery Root with Rosemary-Honey Butter

**SERVES 4** / **PREP TIME:** 10 minutes / **COOK TIME:** 20 minutes

**2 large celery roots, peeled and cut into 1-inch-thick rounds**

**1 tablespoon extra-virgin olive oil**

**Salt**

**2 tablespoons melted salted butter**

**2 teaspoons honey**

**1 to 2 teaspoons chopped fresh rosemary**

1. Preheat the oven to 400°F. Line a baking sheet with parchment paper.

2. On the prepared baking sheet, brush the celery roots with the olive oil. Season with salt.

3. Arrange the celery roots in a single layer.

4. Transfer the baking sheet to the oven. Bake for 15 to 20 minutes, or until the celery roots are tender. Remove from the oven.

5. In a small bowl, mix together the butter, honey, and rosemary.

6. Drizzle the mixture over the rounds just before serving.

# Garlicky Celery Root and Potato Soup

**SERVES 4** / **PREP TIME:** 10 minutes / **COOK TIME:** 30 minutes

*Made with two hearty root vegetables and a roasted garlic bulb, this simple but flavorful soup is a great way to warm up in the winter.*

**1 tablespoon extra-virgin olive oil**

**1 yellow onion, diced**

**1 large celery root, peeled and diced; stalks or leaves chopped, for garnish**

**1 Russet potato, peeled and diced**

**4 cups vegetable broth**

**Salt**

**Freshly ground black pepper**

**1 roasted garlic bulb**
(see page 133)

**¼ cup full-fat plain Greek yogurt**

1. In a large stockpot or Dutch oven, warm the olive oil over high heat.

2. Add the onion, and sauté for 3 to 4 minutes, or until translucent and soft.

3. Add the celery root, potato, and broth. Bring to a boil.

4. Reduce the heat to medium-low. Cover, and cook for 20 to 25 minutes, or until the vegetables are tender. Remove from the heat. Season with salt and pepper.

5. Squeeze the roasted garlic cloves out of the bulb and into the soup. Stir well.

6. Using an immersion blender, puree the soup. Season with salt and pepper to taste.

7. Ladle the soup into bowls, dollop with the Greek yogurt, and garnish with chopped celery root stalks or leaves. Serve hot.

**NOTE:** If you have celery root that does not have its stalks, serve the soup with another fresh herb (likes chopped fresh chives or parsley) instead. If you don't own an immersion blender, see page 27 for notes on making this in a regular blender.

# Chard

**Season:** spring, fall, winter

**Flavor profile:** Chard leaves are earthy and slightly bittersweet, with a taste similar to spinach and beets. They are firm and tough, but less so than kale and collard greens. All parts of chard are edible, and some consider the stems to be sweeter than the leaves.

**Pairs with:** onion, garlic, red wine vinegar, balsamic vinegar, lemon, red pepper flakes, maple syrup, mint, eggs, feta cheese

**Varieties:** Swiss chard (green leaves and white stems) and rainbow chard (yellow, red, white, and orange veins and stems)

**Preparation:** Rinse the leaves under cold running water, and pat dry with clean towels. Use a sharp knife to cut off the leaves from the center stems, then cut the leaves into strips and cut the stems.

**Favorite ways to serve:** raw, sautéed, mixed into eggs, salads, and grain dishes for color and flavor

**Nutritional info:** Chard is rich in potassium, magnesium, and calcium, three nutrients that play a pivotal role in maintaining healthy blood pressure.

It also provides fiber and high amounts of vitamins A and K.

**Selection:** Chard leaves should be vibrant and dark green with bright stems. They should not be wilted, and the stems should not look dried out. To test if chard is fresh, rub your fingers on a leaf to determine if it is still firm and smooth.

**Storage:** The best way to store chard is in a plastic bag in the refrigerator for up to one week. Be sure to squeeze out as much air as possible before sealing the bag.

# Maple Chard Salad

**SERVES 4 / PREP TIME:** 5 minutes

3 tablespoons extra-virgin
  olive oil

2 tablespoons apple
  cider vinegar

2 tablespoons
  maple syrup

2 teaspoons
  whole-grain mustard

1 bunch chard, leaves
  cut into strips,
  stems chopped

1. In a large bowl, whisk together the olive oil, vinegar, maple syrup, and mustard.

2. Add the chard, and toss until evenly coated.

# Rainbow Chard Frittata

**SERVES 4** / **PREP TIME:** 10 minutes / **COOK TIME:** 15 minutes

*Add some color to your breakfast with a vibrant egg dish. This delicious frittata is speckled with colorful rainbow chard stems and leaves, creamy goat cheese, and fresh chives, bringing you sweet, tangy, and savory flavors in every slice. Considering how tasty and easy they are, vegetable-loaded frittatas also make for a great dinner option for busy nights.*

**1 tablespoon extra-virgin olive oil**

**1 sweet onion, diced**

**1 bunch rainbow chard, leaves cut into strips, stems chopped**

**Salt**

**Freshly ground black pepper**

**6 large eggs, beaten**

**2 tablespoons chopped fresh chives**

**¼ cup crumbled vegetarian goat cheese**

1. Turn the broiler to high.

2. In a large cast-iron or oven-safe skillet, warm the olive oil over medium heat.

3. Add the onion and chard. Cook for 4 to 6 minutes, or until tender. Season with salt and pepper.

4. Pour in the eggs, and gently tilt the skillet to distribute evenly.

5. Sprinkle the chives and goat cheese on top. Cook for 2 to 3 minutes, or until the eggs set on the bottom.

6. Transfer the skillet to the oven, and broil for 3 to 5 minutes, or until the eggs are cooked through. Remove from the oven.

**NOTE:** Remember to use oven mitts as needed when handling the skillet to avoid burns. You can substitute ½ to 1 cup caramelized onions (see page 191) in place of the sweet onion for more flavor.

# Baked Chard Risotto

**SERVES 6** / **PREP TIME:** 10 minutes / **COOK TIME:** 50 minutes

*One of my favorite hacks for making a creamy risotto without constant stirring is baking it in the oven. Just place prepped ingredients in a large Dutch oven, cover, and let the oven do the work for you. If this sounds too good to be true, it only gets better with the addition of sweet and earthy chard toward the end of the cooking process.*

**2 tablespoons extra-virgin olive oil**

**1 sweet onion, diced**

**3 garlic cloves, minced**

**4 cups vegetable broth, plus more as needed**

**1½ cups Arborio rice**

**1 bunch chard, leaves and stems chopped**

**1 cup freshly grated vegetarian parmesan cheese**

**1 tablespoon freshly squeezed lemon juice, plus more as needed**

**Grated lemon zest, for serving**

1. Preheat the oven to 375°F.

2. In a Dutch oven, warm the olive oil over medium heat.

3. Add the onion and garlic. Cook for 5 minutes, or until softened.

4. Add the broth. Increase the heat to medium-high and bring to a boil. Remove from the heat.

5. Stir in the rice and cover.

6. Carefully place the Dutch oven on the center rack of the oven and bake for 40 to 45 minutes. The rice should be tender but may appear slightly dry. Remove from the oven.

7. Stir in the chard, parmesan cheese, and lemon juice. Stir vigorously with a wooden spoon for 1 to 2 minutes. Add more broth as needed, and continue to stir until the risotto is moist and at your desired consistency. Taste and add more lemon juice as needed.

8. Serve the risotto with lemon zest.

**NOTE:** If you don't have a Dutch oven, you can use a well-greased 9-by-13-inch baking dish or a casserole dish. In a saucepan, cook the onion and garlic in the olive oil over medium-high heat, add the broth, and bring to a boil. Put the rice in the baking dish and pour the boiling mixture over it. Cover tightly with an oven-safe lid or aluminum foil and continue the recipe as instructed.

# Chicories

**Season:** fall, winter

**Flavor profile:** The chicory family includes a variety of colorful, leafy vegetables that look similar to lettuces. They generally have a bittersweet taste, with escarole and frisée being less bitter than radicchio and Belgian endive. Unless you are particularly fond of this taste, it's best to pair chicories with ingredients that subdue their bitterness and bring out a softer flavor.

**Pairs with:** citrus, balsamic vinegar, red or white wine vinegar, dried fruit, garlic, onion, honey or other sweeteners, salty cheeses like blue, feta, and parmesan

**Varieties:** radicchio (dark purple or red leaves with white veins), escarole (green, looks similar to romaine lettuce), frisée (thin, "frizzy" leaves that are green and yellow), Belgian endive (page 121)

**Preparation:** Best techniques depend on the specific chicory, but you can wash all varieties under cold running water to clean. Use a sharp knife to trim off the ends and chop as desired.

**Favorite ways to serve:** raw, sautéed, roasted

**Nutritional info:** Chicories are generally low in calories and provide an abundance of vitamins and minerals. Most varieties are high in vitamin K, and some are also rich in folate and vitamins A and C.

**Selection:** Similar to selecting any leafy vegetable, look for heads with fresh leaves that are not wilted or discolored.

**Storage:** Loosely wrap escarole, radicchio, or frisée in a damp paper towel, and keep in a plastic bag in the refrigerator to use within a few days.

# Roasted Radicchio with Blue Cheese and Dates

**SERVES 4** / **PREP TIME:** 5 minutes / **COOK TIME:** 25 minutes

**1 head radicchio, quartered**

**1 tablespoon extra-virgin olive oil**

**Salt**

**Freshly ground black pepper**

**8 to 10 pitted medjool dates, thinly sliced**

**½ cup crumbled vegetarian blue cheese**

1. Preheat the oven to 450°F. Line a baking sheet with aluminum foil.

2. Place the radicchio, cut-side down, on the prepared baking sheet.

3. Drizzle the radicchio with the olive oil. Season with salt and pepper.

4. Transfer the baking sheet to the oven and roast for 15 minutes.

5. Flip the radicchio and roast for 5 minutes, or until tender and browned. Remove from the oven.

6. Push the radicchio into the center of the baking sheet.

7. Sprinkle the dates and blue cheese on top.

8. Return the baking sheet to the oven and bake for 3 to 4 minutes, or until the cheese is melted and bubbling. Remove from the oven.

# Frisée Breakfast Salad

**SERVES 4** / **PREP TIME:** 5 minutes / **COOK TIME:** 10 minutes

*Imagine sipping coffee and enjoying this breakfast salad while sitting outside a quaint café with a red-and-white striped awning. If this sounds like a scene from a French bistro to you, you're not mistaken. A simple frisée salad is one of the staple items on bistro menus all across France. But you don't have to travel to Europe to enjoy this dish. You can make the delicious combination of bitter frisée tossed in a mustard-tarragon dressing and topped with a runny egg in your own home.*

**3 tablespoons extra-virgin olive oil**

**2 tablespoons white wine vinegar**

**1 tablespoon Dijon mustard**

**1 tablespoon chopped fresh tarragon**

**1 head frisée, coarsely torn**

**Butter or cooking oil of choice**

**4 large eggs**

**Salt**

**Freshly ground black pepper**

1.  In a large bowl, whisk together the olive oil, vinegar, mustard, and tarragon.

2.  Add the frisée, and toss to combine. Divide equally among serving plates.

3.  In a skillet, warm a little bit of butter or cooking oil over medium heat.

4.  Add the eggs, and cook to your liking, either sunny-side up or over easy. Remove from the heat.

5.  Top the salads with the eggs. Season with salt and pepper to taste.

**NOTE:** Frisée salads typically feature chopped bacon and make use of the bacon renderings in the dressing. For a vegetarian addition that mimics bacon, cut up a few pieces of Eggplant Bacon (page 120) to scatter on top.

# Escarole and White Bean Soup

**SERVES 4 / PREP TIME:** 10 minutes / **COOK TIME:** 20 minutes

*Escarole and white beans are a common culinary pair, but I wasn't aware of how delicious they could be together until I tasted them in soup form. The bittersweet flavor of escarole is perfectly complemented by creamy white beans, garlic, and a pinch of red pepper flakes in this healthy recipe. With such a short cook time and ingredient list, escarole and bean soup will become a new favorite in no time.*

**1 tablespoon extra-virgin olive oil**

**1 yellow onion, diced**

**4 garlic cloves, minced**

**1 tablespoon fresh thyme leaves**

**¼ teaspoon red pepper flakes**

**Salt**

**Freshly ground black pepper**

**1 head escarole, coarsely chopped**

**4 cups vegetable broth**

**1 (15-ounce) can cannellini beans, drained and rinsed**

**Freshly grated vegetarian parmesan cheese, for serving**

1. In a large pot or Dutch oven, warm the olive oil over medium heat.

2. Add the onion, garlic, thyme, and red pepper flakes. Season with salt and pepper. Cook for about 5 minutes, or until the onion has softened and the seasonings are fragrant.

3. Stir in the escarole, broth, and beans. Bring to a gentle boil. Cook, stirring occasionally, for 15 minutes. Using the back of a wooden spoon, mash about half of the beans in the pot. This makes the soup creamier and helps it thicken. Remove from the heat.

4. Serve the soup with freshly grated parmesan cheese.

**NOTE:** If you have one on hand, add a small parmesan rind to the soup while it cooks for even more flavor. Remove before eating. Other possible additions include fresh lemon juice and crusty bread for serving.

# Corn

**Season:** summer

**Flavor profile:** Corn has a sweet taste and a soft, buttery texture, although the flavor profile can be more or less sweet depending on the variety. Raw corn tends to be starchier and less sweet than cooked.

**Pairs with:** butter, sour cream, salt, fresh herbs, peppers, chili powder, potatoes, stone fruit, tomatoes, farro, rice

**Varieties:** sweet corn, dent or field corn (used for animal feed and industrial corn products), flint corn (hard kernels in variety of colors, mostly ornamental)

**Preparation:** Remove the husks and underlying silk that may get stuck on the cob. Trim off the ends with a sharp knife if cooking whole, or use a serrated knife to easily cut off the kernels.

**Favorite ways to serve:** boiled, grilled, raw

**Nutritional info:** In addition to being high in fiber and B vitamins, corn provides a variety of beneficial plant compounds. Two of these compounds, lutein and zeaxanthin, make up a large part of the eye and promote proper eye health.

**Selection:** The husks of fresh corn are tightly wrapped around the cob and should feel slightly moist. Although you may think that brown or sticky silk at the top of husks (the tassel) is a bad sign, this is normal. But if the tassel is black, dry, or mushy, the corn is likely old.

**Storage:** Store corn in their husks in a sealed plastic bag in the produce drawer in the refrigerator. Use within a few days.

# Sautéed Corn with Cinnamon-Honey Butter

**SERVES 4** / **PREP TIME:** 10 minutes / **COOK TIME:** 10 minutes

**1 tablespoon extra-virgin olive oil**

**2 cups fresh sweet corn kernels**

**2 tablespoons unsalted butter, at room temperature**

**1 tablespoon honey**

**¼ teaspoon ground cinnamon**

**Salt**

1. In a large skillet, warm the olive oil over medium heat.

2. Add the corn, and cook, stirring occasionally, for 5 to 7 minutes, or until tender. Remove from the heat.

3. In a small bowl, using a hand mixer, blend together the butter, honey, and cinnamon.

4. Serve the corn with a pat of the cinnamon-honey butter. Season with salt to taste.

# Sweet Corn Risotto

**SERVES 4** / **PREP TIME:** 10 minutes / **COOK TIME:** 30 to 35 minutes

*I'm a fan of any and all risottos, but this variation may just be my favorite. This dish is not only creamy and decadent from a few simple ingredients, but also prominent with the sweet flavor and buttery texture of corn in every bite. Remember to pour yourself a glass of the white wine you use in the recipe to enjoy with this gourmet dish on a warm summer evening.*

**4 cups vegetable broth**
**1 tablespoon extra-virgin olive oil**
**2 shallots, diced**
**1 cup Arborio rice**
**½ cup dry white wine, such as Sauvignon Blanc**
**Salt**
**Freshly ground black pepper**
**2 cups fresh sweet corn kernels**
**1 cup freshly grated vegetarian parmesan cheese**
**2 tablespoons chopped fresh parsley**

1. In a saucepan, bring the broth to a gentle simmer over medium heat. You want it to be hot, but not boiling when you add it to the risotto.

2. In a large pot or Dutch oven, warm the olive oil over medium heat.

3. Add the shallots to the large pot, and cook for 4 to 6 minutes, or until tender.

4. Stir in the rice, and cook, stirring frequently, for 4 minutes, or until translucent.

5. Pour in the white wine, and stir constantly until absorbed by the rice. Season with salt and pepper.

6. Using a soup ladle or a measuring cup, pour ½ cup of the hot broth into the pot, and cook, stirring constantly, until the broth has been absorbed.

7. Continue adding the broth. When half has been added, add the corn. Continue adding the broth, ½ cup at a time, until all of the broth has been added. This step typically takes 20 to 25 minutes, and the rice should be tender and the corn should be cooked at the end of this step. Remove from the heat.

8. Stir in the parmesan cheese and parsley. Season with salt and pepper to taste.

NOTE: Remember to constantly stir the risotto, and do not leave it unattended for more than 60 seconds. Substitute canned or frozen corn if you do not have fresh on hand. Store leftovers in an airtight container in the refrigerator for up to 4 days.

# Boiled Corn on the Cob: Elote Style

**SERVES 4 / PREP TIME:** 10 minutes / **COOK TIME:** 10 minutes

*Mexican street corn, known in Spanish as elote, is a delicious style of corn on the cob smothered in sour cream, chili powder, lime juice, and cotija cheese. I prefer to eat it straight off the cob, but if you have the patience, you can cut off the coated kernels with a serrated knife and eat the dish with a fork. After trying elote, you may never want to eat corn on the cob any other way again. Trust me.*

**4 ears fresh sweet corn, husked**

**¼ cup sour cream**

**Juice of ½ lime**

**¼ cup crumbled cotija cheese** (see notes)

**2 teaspoons chili powder**

**2 tablespoons chopped fresh cilantro**

**½ lime, cut into wedges**

**Salt**

1. Bring a large pot of salted water to a boil.

2. Add the corn, and cook for 6 to 8 minutes, or until the kernels are tender. Remove from the heat.

3. In a shallow bowl, mix together the sour cream, lime juice, cotija cheese, and chili powder.

4. Using tongs, remove the ears of corn from the pot. Rub each ear of corn in the sour cream mixture, making sure to cover the entire ear.

5. Sprinkle the corn with the cilantro, and serve with lime wedges. Make sure to have extra napkins; you'll need them.

**NOTE:** Cotija cheese is typically made with animal rennet. If this is a concern, as an alternative, you can use vegetarian parmesan cheese, which is made with microbial or vegetarian rennet. You can also substitute full-fat plain Greek yogurt or crema fresca for the sour cream. For a spicier kick, add a dash of cayenne pepper.

# Fresh Corn and Cherry Dip

**MAKES ABOUT 4 CUPS / PREP TIME:** 15 minutes

*The fresh flavors in this corn and cherry dip are a perfect match for tortilla chips, but you can also serve it on top of grilled summer squash for a light side dish. It's colorful, nutritious, and fun and makes for a great addition to a warm weather cookout or 4th of July spread. Depending on where you live, cherry and corn season may overlap for a short (and magical) period of time. But if you can't find one of the main ingredients fresh, frozen or canned varieties work just as well.*

**2 cups fresh sweet corn kernels**

**2 cups cherries, pitted and thinly sliced**

**½ cup diced red onion**

**2 tablespoons fresh basil chiffonade**

**2 tablespoons chopped fresh mint**

**Juice of 1 lemon**

**Salt**

**Tortilla chips or pita chips, for serving**

In a medium bowl, combine the corn, cherries, onion, basil, mint, and lemon juice. Stir well. Season with salt to taste. Serve with tortilla chips or pita chips.

**NOTE:** To pit fresh cherries, insert a reusable, stainless steel straw into the center of each cherry to gently pop out the pit.

# Cucumbers

**Season:** summer

**Flavor profile:** Cucumbers have a distinct crispness with a light, slightly sweet, and sometimes bitter flavor. Their taste may also be described as hydrating, since they have high water content and fairly juicy flesh.

**Pairs with:** onion, tomatoes, fresh fruit, yogurt, sour cream, vinegars, citrus, dill, black pepper

**Varieties:** garden cucumbers (large seeds), English cucumbers (seedless), pickling (Kirby) cucumbers, gherkins (very small)

**Preparation:** Wash cucumbers under cold running water, using your hands or a vegetable brush to rub the skin clean. Use a swivel peeler to remove the skin

if desired. To remove the seeds, cut the cucumber into quarters lengthwise and then make a thin slice down the center of each quarter to remove the seeds.

**Favorite ways to serve:** raw, pickled

**Nutritional info:** Cucumbers are more than 96 percent water and can help contribute to daily water intake. They provide vitamins C and K, potassium, manganese, and several compounds that may act as antioxidants and prevent damage to cells in the body.

**Selection:** Choose cucumbers that are firm with bright green skin, free of blemishes or indications of rotting.

**Storage:** Wrap cucumbers tightly with plastic wrap, or place them in paper towels in a sealed plastic bag. Store in the produce drawer in the refrigerator for up to one week.

# Homemade Refrigerator Pickles

**MAKES 1 PINT / PREP TIME:** 10 minutes, plus 24 hours to chill / **COOK TIME:** 15 minutes

3 pickling cucumbers, cut lengthwise into about 12 spears

½ sweet onion, thinly sliced

6 fresh dill sprigs

½ cup apple cider vinegar

3 garlic cloves, smashed

1 teaspoon sugar

1½ teaspoons salt

¼ teaspoon whole black peppercorns

1. Stuff the cucumbers, onion, and dill into a pint jar with a lid.

2. In a small saucepan, combine the vinegar, garlic, sugar, salt, peppercorns, and ½ cup of water. Warm over medium heat for 3 to 5 minutes, or until the salt and sugar dissolve. Remove from the heat. Let cool for 10 to 15 minutes.

3. Pour the brine into the jar, and seal tightly. Refrigerate for at least 24 hours before eating.

# Simple Cucumber-Yogurt Sauce

**MAKES ABOUT 2½ CUPS / PREP TIME:** 10 minutes

*I first discovered cucumber-yogurt sauce, also known as tzatziki, at a Greek restaurant when I lived in Philadelphia. Not only did I find the cool and creamy flavor irresistible, but also I was amazed at the versatility of this condiment. From serving as a veggie dip to sandwich spread and all-purpose sauce, this recipe knows no bounds. Fortunately, it's so easy to whip up and keep in the refrigerator for everyday use.*

**2 cups full-fat plain Greek yogurt**

**1 cup cucumber, peeled, seeded, and diced (1 small cucumber)**

**Juice of ½ lemon**

**1 tablespoon dried dill or 3 tablespoons chopped fresh**

**½ teaspoon salt**

**Freshly ground black pepper**

In a small bowl, mix together the yogurt, cucumber, lemon juice, dill, and salt. It should be creamy and slightly chunky. Season with pepper to taste.

**NOTE:** Store this sauce in an airtight container or glass jar in the refrigerator for up to 1 week. Use as a dip for chopped carrots, celery, bell peppers, and radishes, or as a spread for vegetable sandwiches and wraps. You can also mix it into grain bowls.

# Spicy Cucumber, Cashew, and Edamame Salad

**SERVES 4 / PREP TIME:** 10 minutes

*With their refreshing, cool taste and crunchy texture, cucumbers are an ideal counterpart to a spicy dressing. Chopped cashews add a nutty undertone and a source of healthy fats, while edamame contributes plant-based protein. This balanced dish can be served as a main or a side, and is a good option to prep in advance for lunch.*

**FOR THE DRESSING**

- 2 tablespoons sriracha
- 1 tablespoon extra-virgin olive oil
- 1 tablespoon rice vinegar
- 1 teaspoon honey
- 2 garlic cloves, minced

**FOR THE SALAD**

- 1 large cucumber, peeled, seeded, and diced
- ¾ cup cooked edamame
- ½ cup chopped dry-roasted cashews
- 2 tablespoons chopped fresh cilantro

**TO MAKE THE DRESSING**

1. In a medium bowl, whisk together the sriracha, olive oil, vinegar, honey, and garlic.

**TO MAKE THE SALAD**

2. Add the cucumber, edamame, cashews, and cilantro. Toss until evenly coated.

**NOTE:** Store in the refrigerator in an airtight container for up to four days. Possible additions include sesame seeds, chopped fresh mint, or a squeeze of lime juice.

# Cucumber-Melon Fruit Salsa

**MAKES ABOUT 4 CUPS / PREP TIME:** 15 minutes

*Cucumbers are a headliner vegetable (well, technically a fruit) of summer. Many home gardeners find themselves swimming in cukes by the middle of the season. If you find yourself in that pickle (pun intended), this sweet yet spicy salsa is for you. Made with cucumber and cantaloupe in place of tomatoes, it's a wonderfully fresh and colorful snack. Pair it with tortilla chips for an afternoon treat, or serve it over grilled vegetables and tofu.*

**1 garden cucumber, peeled and diced**

**½ cantaloupe, peeled, seeded, and diced**

**½ cup chopped red onion**

**1 jalapeño pepper, seeded and finely chopped**

**Juice of 1 lemon**

**2 tablespoons chopped fresh cilantro, plus more as needed**

**1 tablespoon extra-virgin olive oil**

**Salt**

**Freshly ground black pepper**

1. In a medium bowl, mix together the cucumber, cantaloupe, onion, and jalapeño.

2. Add the lemon juice, cilantro, and olive oil. Stir well. Season with salt and pepper to taste.

**NOTE:** You can serve this salsa immediately with tortilla chips or pita chips, but it tastes especially delicious after sitting in the refrigerator for about 1 hour to let the flavors meld.

# Eggplant

**Season:** summer

**Flavor profile:** Eggplants, also known as aubergines, have deep purple skin with tan flesh that has brown spots surrounding the seeds. Known for its spongy texture, eggplant can soak up flavors very well. However, its taste alone is bland and slightly bitter.

**Pairs with:** onion, tomato, zucchini, bell pepper, basil, oregano, parsley, garlic, soy sauce, parmesan cheese

**Varieties:** globe (big and plump), Japanese (thin and long), rosa bianca (purple and white streaked skin), white

**Preparation:** To reduce the bitterness of its flesh, eggplant slices are often sprinkled with salt and left to sit until they begin to "sweat." This practice helps draw out moisture and any unpleasant tastes along with it.

**Favorite ways to serve:** grilled, sautéed, braised, roasted, breaded

**Nutritional info:** Eggplants not only offer vitamins, minerals, and fiber but also contain anthocyanin pigments that are responsible for their colorful skin. Consumption of anthocyanins has been associated with possible anti-cancer effects.

**Selection:** To test the freshness of an eggplant, gently press your thumb into the skin to ensure that it is firm and not squishy. Inspect the skin, and choose shiny eggplants that do not have bruises.

**Storage:** Fresh eggplant is best stored at room temperature in a cool, dry area that does not get direct sunlight. Keep it away from bananas and melons, or transfer it to a plastic bag and keep in the refrigerator.

# Classic Eggplant Parmesan

**SERVES 4 TO 6 / PREP TIME:** 15 minutes / **COOK TIME:** 40 minutes

*This widely loved dish is an easy vegetarian main course that you can put together with basic pantry ingredients. Whether you enjoy it during peak eggplant season in the summer or for a warm dinner on a cold evening, it's comforting, familiar, and downright delicious. Degorging the eggplant with salt is optional in this recipe and can be skipped if you're short on time.*

**2 medium eggplants, cut into ½-inch-thick rounds**

**½ teaspoon salt, plus more if degorging the eggplant**

**2 large eggs**

**1½ cups plain bread crumbs**

**1 teaspoon dried oregano**

**1 teaspoon dried basil**

**1 (24-ounce) jar tomato sauce of choice or Homemade Tomato Sauce** (page 251)**, divided**

**1½ cups shredded vegetarian mozzarella cheese, divided**

**½ cup freshly grated vegetarian parmesan cheese, divided**

**Chopped fresh basil** (optional)

1. If degorging, sprinkle the eggplant slices liberally with salt, and place them in a colander set over a bowl or in the sink for 30 minutes. Rinse and pat dry with paper towels.

2. Preheat the oven to 400°F. Line 2 baking sheets with parchment paper. Grease a 9-by-13-inch baking dish.

3. Beat the eggs in a bowl large enough to accommodate dipping the eggplant rounds.

4. In a separate shallow bowl, combine the bread crumbs, ½ teaspoon of salt, the oregano, and basil.

5. Dip each eggplant round in the eggs and then in the bread crumb mixture, making sure to flip with a fork to coat both sides.

6. Arrange the eggplants in a single layer on the prepared baking sheets.

7. Transfer the baking sheets to the oven, and bake for 15 minutes, flipping halfway through. Remove from the oven.

8. Spread ½ cup of tomato sauce in the prepared baking dish.

9. Arrange a layer of eggplant rounds, followed by 1 cup of tomato sauce.

10. Sprinkle ¾ cup of mozzarella cheese and ¼ cup of parmesan cheese on top. Repeat this step with another layer of eggplant rounds, the remaining sauce, ¾ cup of mozzarella cheese, and ¼ cup of parmesan cheese.

11. Transfer the baking dish to the oven, and bake for 20 to 25 minutes, or until the cheese is melted and bubbly. Remove from the oven.

12. Sprinkle the eggplant parm with fresh basil (if using) and serve.

NOTE: Serve with steamed broccoli, green beans, or a side salad. You can also make eggplant parm sandwiches by spooning portions into toasted sub or hoagie rolls.

# Simple Grilled Eggplant

**SERVES 4 / PREP TIME:** 5 minutes, plus 30 minutes to degorge / **COOK TIME:** 10 minutes

**2 medium eggplants, cut into ¾-inch-thick slices**
**Salt**
**¼ cup extra-virgin olive oil**
**Freshly ground black pepper**

1. Sprinkle both sides of the eggplant slices liberally with salt. Let sit in a colander set over a bowl or in the sink for 30 minutes, or until they start to "sweat" out their bitter juices. Rinse and pat dry with paper towels.

2. Preheat the grill on medium-high heat.

3. Brush each side of the eggplant slices with the olive oil. Season with salt and pepper.

4. Place the eggplant directly on the grill or on a vegetable mat on the grill, and grill for 4 to 5 minutes on each side, or until the flesh is tender and the skin is slightly charred. It's best to keep grill times short to avoid overcooking and making the eggplant mushy. Remove from the heat.

# Braised Eggplant Shakshuka

**SERVES 4** / **PREP TIME:** 10 minutes / **COOK TIME:** 25 to 30 minutes

*Shakshuka is an incredibly flavorful, stew-like dish made from tomatoes, spices, and herbs and topped with eggs. It's widely popular in Middle Eastern, North African, and Mediterranean countries, although its popularity in the United States is growing thanks to its complex flavor profile and simple preparation. This rendition features braised eggplant for some additional texture and flavor.*

**2 tablespoons extra-virgin olive oil**

**1 yellow onion, diced**

**3 garlic cloves, minced**

**1 medium eggplant, diced**

**2 teaspoons smoked paprika**

**1 teaspoon ground cumin**

**¼ teaspoon chili powder**

**Salt**

**1 (28-ounce) can whole peeled tomatoes**

**4 large eggs**

**½ cup chopped fresh parsley**

1. In a large skillet, warm the olive oil over medium heat.

2. Add the onion, garlic, and eggplant. Cook for 6 to 8 minutes, or until tender.

3. Add the paprika, cumin, and chili powder. Season with salt. Cook, stirring, for 2 to 3 minutes, or until the spices are fragrant.

4. Add the tomatoes with their juices.

5. Reduce the heat to medium-low. Cook for 10 minutes, or until the vegetables have softened and tomato juices have started to evaporate. The pan will be crowded. Using the back of a wooden spoon, gently crush the tomatoes as they cook.

6. Make 4 wells in the mixture and crack an egg into each one. Cover the skillet and cook for 5 to 7 minutes, or until the eggs reach your desired consistency. Remove from the heat.

7. Garnish the shakshuka with the parsley, and serve.

**NOTE:** Possible additions include chopped fresh cilantro and crumbled vegetarian feta cheese. You can also serve the shakshuka with warm pita or crunchy bread.

# Eggplant Bacon

**SERVES 6** / **PREP TIME:** 10 minutes / **COOK TIME:** 20 minutes

*This plant-based twist on bacon offers a similar smoky and salty flavor profile and makes for a great addition to vegetarian BLTs and breakfast sandwiches. If you want to take it a step further and mimic the crispiness of true bacon, cut the eggplant as thin as possible. I even went so far as to pull out a ruler to help me make perfect 1/16-inch slices, and it made all the difference. A mandoline can come in handy for this recipe but is not required.*

**4 tablespoons extra-virgin olive oil, divided**
**2 tablespoons soy sauce**
**1 tablespoon maple syrup**
**1 teaspoon smoked paprika**
**1 teaspoon vegan Worcestershire sauce**
**1 medium eggplant, cut into 1/16-inch-thick slices**

1. Line a plate with paper towels. In a small bowl, whisk together 2 tablespoons of olive oil, the soy sauce, maple syrup, paprika, and Worcestershire sauce.

2. Brush each slice of eggplant on both sides with the mixture. Transfer to a plate.

3. In a large skillet, warm the remaining 2 tablespoons of olive oil over medium heat until fragrant.

4. Arrange the eggplant slices in a single layer in the skillet (you will likely have to cook them in batches), and cook, gently flipping with tongs, for 4 to 5 minutes on each side, or until slightly charred and crispy. Keep a close eye on the eggplant to make sure it doesn't burn. The next batches will take less time as the skillet heats up. Transfer to the paper towel–lined plate. The eggplant will continue to crisp up as it cools. Enjoy immediately.

**NOTE:** This bacon is definitely crispiest when eaten right away, but it can be stored in an airtight container in the refrigerator for up to 3 days.

# Endive

**Season:** fall, winter

**Flavor profile:** Belgian endive has a cylindrical shape with narrow, tightly-packed leaves that have yellow or purple-red tips and a white base. A type of chicory, it has a crunchy texture and subtle bitterness that can be mellowed by cooking methods and flavor pairings.

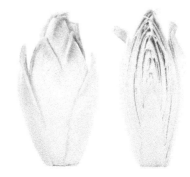

**Pairs with:** citrus, dried fruits, apples, garlic, sunflower seeds, pistachios, and feta, blue, or goat cheeses

**Varieties:** just one, but can have yellow or red leaves

**Preparation:** Trim off the end, and cut in half or into thin slices. Separate the leaves with your hands if you intend to keep them whole.

**Favorite ways to serve:** braised, raw

**Nutritional info:** Belgian endive is rich in fiber that can promote optimal digestion and regular bowel movements. It's also a good source of bone-strengthening vitamin K.

**Selection:** Endive leaves should cling together and appear firm. Discolored or wilted leaf tips are an indication that the vegetable is old and has almost gone bad.

**Storage:** Since endive likes the dark, wrap it in paper towels before placing it in a plastic bag to store in the refrigerator. It can last in the produce drawer for up to a week and sometimes a bit longer.

# Braised Endive

**SERVES 4** / **PREP TIME:** 5 minutes / **COOK TIME:** 30 minutes

**2 tablespoons extra-virgin olive oil**

**4 to 6 heads Belgian endive, trimmed**

**Juice of 1 lemon**

**½ cup vegetable broth**

**5 or 6 fresh thyme sprigs**

1. In a pot or Dutch oven, warm the olive oil over medium heat.

2. Nestle the endive in the pot in a single layer.

3. Add the lemon juice, broth, and thyme.

4. Reduce the heat to low. Cover and simmer for about 30 minutes, or until tender. Remove from the heat.

# Stuffed Endive with Zesty Goat Cheese

**SERVES 6 / PREP TIME:** 15 minutes

*Stuffed endive leaves make for the perfect appetizer, especially since they can be enjoyed in three bites or less. Herbed goat cheese mixed with lemon zest makes this recipe appear fancy, but it only takes 15 minutes to prepare. Whip it up before your next dinner party to wow your guests with a unique and delicious vegetable that may be unfamiliar to them.*

½ cup crumbled vegetarian goat cheese

1 tablespoon freshly squeezed lemon juice

½ teaspoon grated lemon zest, plus more as needed

2 tablespoons thinly sliced fresh chives

1 tablespoon chopped fresh parsley

Salt

Freshly ground black pepper

18 to 24 Belgian endive leaves (about 2 heads)

1. In a medium bowl, using a fork, mash together the goat cheese, lemon juice, lemon zest, chives, and parsley. Season with salt and pepper to taste.

2. Stuff the endive leaves with the goat cheese mixture, arrange on a serving plate, and serve immediately.

**NOTE:** Possible additions include fresh mint or tarragon, chopped walnuts, or small pieces of fresh pear or apple.

# Fava Beans

**Season:** spring

**Flavor profile:** Fava beans, also known as broad beans, come in large green pods. The beans are removed from their pods before cooking and eating. When properly prepared, they have a buttery and slightly nutty taste that's often described as spring-like.

**Pairs with:** peas, artichokes, mint, tomato, onions, garlic, olive oil, salt, most nuts, and feta, goat, or parmesan cheeses

**Varieties:** can vary in shape, size, and color

**Preparation:** Unzip the bean pods to remove the beans. To get rid of the waxy skin that surrounds each bean, blanch the beans in boiling water for 30 to 60 seconds, and transfer them to an ice bath. The skin will be easy to peel after this process. One pound of bean pods yields about one cup of peeled beans.

**Favorite ways to serve:** steamed, mashed, added to salads or pasta

**Nutritional info:** Fava beans are packed with plant-based protein and contain a high amount of folate, a water-soluble vitamin that's especially important for pregnant women to consume to prevent birth defects.

**Selection:** Choose broad beans that have smooth, bright green pods. You should be able to see bumps from the beans inside but they should not be bulging, which is an indicator that they may be old.

**Storage:** Store fava beans still in their pods in a paper or plastic bag in the refrigerator for up to 10 days. Shelled fava beans can be stored in the freezer for up to 3 months.

# Marinated Fava Beans

**MAKES ABOUT 1 CUP** / **PREP TIME:** 15 minutes, plus 24 hours to marinate /
**COOK TIME:** 1 minute

½ teaspoon salt, plus
   more for blanching
1 pound fava bean pods
¼ cup red wine vinegar
¼ cup extra-virgin olive oil
2 tablespoons chopped
   fresh parsley
2 garlic cloves, minced
¼ teaspoon red
   pepper flakes

1. Bring a pot of salted water to a boil over high heat. Fill a bowl with ice water.

2. Unzip each bean pod to remove the beans. Drop the beans into the boiling water and blanch for 60 to 90 seconds until the beans start to float to the top of the pot. Remove from the heat. Immediately drain, and submerge in the bowl of ice water. (The process of blanching ensures that the beans stay green and fresh.)

3. Drain the beans again, and use your fingers to squeeze each bean and remove the skin.

4. In a 1-pint glass jar, combine the vinegar, olive oil, parsley, garlic, salt, and red pepper flakes. Shake well.

5. Put the fava beans in the jar, seal tightly, and shake to combine. Refrigerate for at least 24 hours before serving.

# Mashed Fava Bean Bruschetta

**SERVES 6** / **PREP TIME:** 15 minutes / **COOK TIME:** 10 minutes

*Vegetal fava beans shine in this spring-inspired bruschetta, complemented by garlic, fresh mint, and lemon. Although the preparation of these beans can be tedious, the mashed fava beans are lusciously creamy and delicious. Make a batch of marinated fava beans a few days in advance so that they have time to soak up the flavors before you prepare this recipe.*

**12 (½-inch-thick) Italian bread or baguette slices**

**1 tablespoon extra-virgin olive oil**

**2 garlic cloves, minced**

**Marinated Fava Beans** (page 125)

**Juice of 1 lemon**

**¼ cup chopped fresh mint**

**Salt**

**Freshly ground black pepper**

1. Turn the broiler to high.

2. Put the bread slices on a baking sheet.

3. In a small bowl, mix together the olive oil and garlic.

4. Brush the mixture onto the bread.

5. Transfer the baking sheet to the oven. Broil for 2 to 3 minutes, or until the bread is lightly toasted. Remove from the oven.

6. Using a slotted spoon, transfer the fava beans to a bowl.

7. Add the lemon juice, and mash the beans with a fork. (Depending on how tender the beans are, they will be more or less difficult to mash.) For a creamier mash, pulse the beans and lemon juice in a food processor instead.

8. Spread a spoonful of the fava mash on the toasted bread.

9. Top the bruschetta with the mint. Season with salt and pepper to taste.

**NOTE:** Possible additions include red pepper flakes, fresh basil, and shaved vegetarian Parmesan cheese.

# Fennel

**Season:** fall, winter

**Flavor profile:** Fennel is a bulbous vegetable with a white base, bright green stalks, and wispy fronds. Though all parts of fennel are edible, typically only the base is used in recipes. It contributes a sweet and subtle licorice flavor.

**Pairs with:** tomato, garlic, onion, carrots, beets, orange, lemon, Granny Smith apple, red wine vinegar, red pepper flakes, hazelnuts

**Varieties:** herb fennel (cultivated for its stems, leaves, and seeds), Florence fennel (grown for its bulb to be eaten as a vegetable)

**Preparation:** Cut off the stalks, fronds, and ends. Cut the bulb into quarters, and remove the core at the bottom of each quarter with a paring or chef's knife.

**Favorite ways to serve:** raw, roasted, braised, seared

**Nutritional info:** In addition to being a good source of fiber and vitamin C, fennel provides manganese. This trace mineral is important for metabolism and blood sugar regulation.

**Selection:** The freshest fennel bulbs are white without any brown spots or bruises. If the stalks and fronds are attached, make sure they look vibrant and do not have any flowers.

**Storage:** Before storing, trim fennel stalks about two inches above the bulb. Keep the bulbs in a sealed plastic bag in the refrigerator for about one week.

# Pan-Seared Fennel

**SERVES 4** / **PREP TIME:** 5 minutes / **COOK TIME:** 10 minutes

1 tablespoon extra-virgin
  olive oil

1 fennel bulb, cored and
  thinly sliced

Juice of ½ lemon

Salt

Freshly ground
  black pepper

1. In a skillet, warm the olive oil over medium heat.

2. Add the fennel, and cook for about 5 minutes on each side, or until browned and tender. Remove from the heat.

3. Add the lemon juice. Season with salt and pepper.

# Fennel, Parsley, and Quinoa Salad

**SERVES 4 / PREP TIME:** 5 minutes

*Licorice-like raw fennel pairs nicely with fresh parsley and a basic lemon-honey dressing in this easy grain salad. Feel free to customize it however you'd like, swapping in farro for the quinoa, adding white beans or lentils for more protein, or mixing in additional fresh herbs like tarragon. Though the structure of this salad is basic, the flavor profile is complex, with hints of anise, zesty citrus, salt, and earthy undertones.*

## FOR THE DRESSING

¼ cup extra-virgin olive oil
Juice of 1 lemon
1 teaspoon Dijon mustard
2 teaspoons honey

## FOR THE SALAD

1 fennel bulb, cored
   and sliced
½ bunch fresh
   parsley, chopped
2 cups cooked quinoa
½ cup crumbled
   vegetarian feta cheese
Salt
Freshly ground
   black pepper

**TO MAKE THE DRESSING**

1. In a medium bowl, whisk together the olive oil, lemon juice, mustard, and honey.

**TO MAKE THE SALAD**

2. Add the fennel, parsley, quinoa, and feta cheese. Toss until well coated. Season with salt and pepper to taste.

NOTE: Store leftovers in an airtight container in the refrigerator for up to 5 days. Cook the quinoa according to the package instructions, and use broth instead of water for more flavor.

# Roasted Fennel and Tomatoes over Pasta

**SERVES 6** / **PREP TIME:** 15 minutes / **COOK TIME:** 30 to 40 minutes

*With their tender texture, flavorful juices, and mouthwatering caramelization, roasted tomatoes are one of my favorite foods. Pairing them with fennel, which gets just as caramelized through roasting, brings this recipe to a whole new level. Be sure to line your baking sheet with foil so that you can easily funnel the tomato and fennel juices onto your plate for maximum flavor. If you find yourself eating the whole tray, don't say I didn't warn you of its deliciousness.*

**2 pounds cherry tomatoes, halved**

**1 fennel bulb, cored and thinly sliced**

**½ sweet onion, thinly sliced**

**3 tablespoons extra-virgin olive oil**

**½ teaspoon dried basil**

**¼ teaspoon dried oregano**

**Salt**

**Freshly ground black pepper**

**6 cups cooked pasta**

1. Preheat the oven to 450°F. Line a baking sheet with aluminum foil.

2. On the prepared baking sheet, using your hands or a rubber spatula, toss the tomatoes, fennel, and onion with the olive oil, basil, and oregano until evenly coated. Season with salt and pepper. The baking sheet will be a little crowded, but that's okay.

3. Transfer the baking sheet to the oven, and roast for 30 to 40 minutes, or until the fennel is tender and the tomatoes have caramelized. Remove from the oven.

4. Serve the vegetables warm over the pasta.

**NOTE:** You can use 1 teaspoon each of chopped fresh oregano and basil instead of dried if available. Add the basil after roasting. For more protein, mix in white beans or chickpeas.

# Garlic

**Season:** summer, fall

**Flavor profile:** Although it is typically considered a seasoning by chefs and home cooks alike, garlic is a vegetable by botanical definition. Garlic bulbs pack several cloves that provide a spicy, strong, sinus-clearing taste that's reminiscent of its relatives: onions, shallots, leeks, and chives.

**Pairs with:** olive oil, most vinegars, citrus, soy sauce, ginger, honey, red pepper flakes, rosemary, thyme, oregano, most fresh herbs

**Varieties:** softnecks (no scapes, smaller in size, white skin), hardnecks (has scapes, can have purple stripes on skin); garlic scapes are also harvested during the summer and can be used in cooking

**Preparation:** Break off the number of cloves you need from the bulb with your hands or with the help of a paring knife. Smash each clove with the side of a chef's knife, or use a silicone garlic roller to help remove the skin. You can then use a garlic press or knife to mince the cloves.

**Favorite ways to serve:** minced or roasted whole and added as a seasoning

**Nutritional info:** Garlic contains a variety of compounds that have been linked to immune-boosting health benefits, lower blood pressure, and a decreased risk of heart disease.

**Selection:** Choose bulbs that are firm without any green shoots sprouting out of the center. There should be no areas that are dark or dried out.

**Storage:** Store whole garlic bulbs at room temperature in a cool, dry area or in a garlic keeper.

# Roasted Garlic Bulbs

**MAKES 2 BULBS / PREP TIME:** 5 minutes / **COOK TIME:** 40 minutes

**2 heads garlic**

**2 tablespoons extra-virgin olive oil**

1. Preheat the oven to 400°F.

2. Remove most of the papery skin surrounding the garlic bulbs, but leave the skin on individual cloves so that the bulb remains intact.

3. Using a sharp knife, cut ½ inch off the top of the cloves.

4. Place each bulb on a square of aluminum foil.

5. Drizzle 1 tablespoon of olive oil onto the cloves of each bulb, using your fingers to rub it over the cut surfaces. Wrap the bulbs in the foil.

6. Transfer the bulbs to the oven, and roast for 30 to 40 minutes, or until soft. Remove from the oven. Let cool.

7. Using a spoon, remove the roasted cloves, or squeeze them out with your fingers.

8. Spread the roasted garlic on bread or add to dressings and marinades.

# Garlic-Infused Honey

**MAKES ABOUT 1½ CUPS / PREP TIME:** 5 minutes, plus at least 3 days to infuse

*Though garlic and honey may seem like an odd pairing, it is the perfect marriage of pungent and mellow. The longer the garlic sits in the jar, the more subdued it becomes as the sweet honey mellows some of its spice. The result is a versatile, delicious condiment that can be used on biscuits and toast or drizzled onto roasted vegetables and corn on the cob. What's more, this fermented food is thought to provide immune-boosting benefits.*

**1 head garlic, cloves separated and peeled**

**1½ cups honey**

1. In a glass jar with a lid, combine the garlic and honey.

2. Seal the jar, and let sit for at least 3 days. At this point, you should see small bubbles forming at the top of the mixture.

3. Open the jar to let any gas escape, give the mixture a stir, and repeat this step every 3 days.

**NOTE:** You can technically use the honey at any point, but the flavor becomes more pronounced the longer you let it sit. It will become runny and thin over time. The garlic honey can be stored for up to three months in a cool, dry place. I typically keep it on a countertop away from direct light or in a cabinet.

# All-Purpose Garlic Marinade

**MAKES ABOUT ½ CUP / PREP TIME:** 5 minutes

*Garlic on its own is an incredibly versatile seasoning that can be used in countless ways. But it's nice to have a go-to garlic marinade that's tried-and-true. This basic recipe features fresh lime juice and mustard that provides just enough zest and tang to complement the garlic. You can also modify it with ingredients you have on hand, such as lemon juice or apple cider vinegar instead of lime juice.*

**¼ cup extra-virgin olive oil**

**Juice of 2 limes**

**4 garlic cloves, minced**

**2 tablespoons whole-grain mustard**

**½ teaspoon salt**

**½ teaspoon freshly ground black pepper**

1. In a glass jar with a lid, combine the olive oil, lime juice, garlic, mustard, salt, and pepper.

2. Seal the lid, and shake well. Use as a salad dressing or to marinate vegetables before grilling.

**NOTE:** Store in the refrigerator for up to 2 weeks. Shake well before using.

# Ginger

**Season:** fall

**Flavor profile:** Ginger, as most home chefs know it, is the bumpy root of a flowering plant that's commonly used as a spice in cooking. Although it's not technically a vegetable, it's vital to preparing flavorful vegetarian meals. It has a strong, spicy flavor.

**Pairs with:** sesame, soy sauce, honey, garlic, peanut butter and peanuts, lime juice, rice vinegar, apple cider vinegar, sugar, molasses, autumnal spices

**Varieties:** several (the most commonly consumed have brown skin and yellow flesh)

**Preparation:** Fresh ginger should be peeled before being used in cooking. You can use a spoon or a swivel peeler and knife to remove the skin.

**Favorite ways to serve:** minced, grated and added to marinades and dressings, candied, used in baked goods

**Nutritional info:** Ginger is widely used as a home remedy for nausea. It has also been shown to fight inflammation and is therefore added to many dishes and products for an anti-inflammatory boost.

**Storage:** Unpeeled ginger can be stored in a sealed plastic bag in the refrigerator for two to three weeks. Wrap any cut surfaces with plastic wrap before storing.

# Soy-Ginger Vinaigrette

**MAKES ABOUT 1 CUP / PREP TIME:** 5 minutes

½ cup extra-virgin
  olive oil

¼ cup rice vinegar

1 tablespoon honey

1 tablespoon finely
  chopped fresh ginger

2 tablespoons soy sauce

2 scallions, green and
  white parts, thinly sliced

1. In a glass jar with a lid, combine the olive oil, vinegar, honey, ginger, soy sauce, and scallions.

2. Seal the lid and shake well. Use on salads or as a marinade for vegetables. The vinaigrette tastes great on zucchini and cucumber noodles.

NOTE: Store the vinaigrette in the refrigerator for up to 2 weeks. Shake well before using. Use maple syrup in place of honey to make it vegan.

# Ginger Switchel

**SERVES 3 / PREP TIME:** 20 minutes, plus 30 minutes to chill

*If you love tangy vinegars and zesty ginger, switchel is bound to become your new favorite drink. This refreshing beverage is made with ginger-infused water, apple cider vinegar, and honey or maple syrup. You can sip it as an afternoon pick-me-up, or use it as a mixer for an alcoholic beverage. Switchel is easy to prep in large batches and store in the refrigerator so that you can get your ginger fix all week long.*

**1 (3-inch) piece fresh ginger, thinly sliced**
**½ cup honey or maple syrup**
**½ cup apple cider vinegar**
**Plain or sparkling water, for serving**

1. In a saucepan, combine the ginger and 2 cups of water. Bring to a boil over medium-high heat. Remove from the heat. Let cool for 15 to 20 minutes.

2. Pour the mixture into a glass jar with a lid.

3. Add the honey and vinegar.

4. Seal the lid, and shake well.

5. Refrigerate for at least 30 minutes. At this point, you can drink the switchel as is, or pour it into a glass with ice, half sparkling water, and half switchel.

NOTE: The longer you let the switchel sit in the refrigerator, the more concentrated and spicy it will become. Depending on your taste preferences, you may want to dilute the switchel with water before drinking.

# Ginger-Molasses Muffins

**MAKES 12 MUFFINS** / **PREP TIME:** 10 minutes / **COOK TIME:** 20 to 25 minutes

*During our first Christmas season as a couple, my husband introduced me to his grandmother's recipe for spice cookies made with molasses. They're rich, perfectly soft, and the most delicious holiday cookies I have ever tasted. Her cookie recipe doesn't call for fresh ginger like this one does, but it's still the inspiration behind these similarly rich "spiced" muffins that use molasses as the primary sweetener.*

**Nonstick cooking spray**
**1½ cups all-purpose flour**
**1 teaspoon baking powder**
**½ teaspoon baking soda**
**½ teaspoon
  ground cinnamon**
**¼ teaspoon
  ground nutmeg**
**¼ teaspoon salt**
**½ cup blackstrap
  molasses**
**½ cup full-fat plain
  Greek yogurt**
**¼ cup packed light
  brown sugar**
**¼ cup canola oil**
**2 large eggs**
**2 tablespoons grated
  fresh ginger**

1. Preheat the oven to 350°F. Spray or line a 12-cup muffin tin.

2. In a medium bowl, mix together the flour, baking powder, baking soda, cinnamon, nutmeg, and salt.

3. In a large bowl, whisk together the molasses, yogurt, sugar, canola oil, eggs, and ginger.

4. Add the dry ingredients to the wet ingredients, and whisk until well combined.

5. Fill each cup in the muffin tin about ⅔ full with the batter.

6. Transfer the muffin tin to the oven, and bake for 18 to 22 minutes, or until a toothpick inserted into the center of a muffin comes out clean. Remove from the oven. Let cool slightly before removing from the tin.

**NOTE:** The muffins taste delicious on their own or with a slab of soft butter or cream cheese. Keep them in an air-tight container at room temperature for up to 5 days.

# Homemade Candied Ginger

**MAKES ABOUT 4 CUPS / PREP TIME:** 10 minutes / **COOK TIME:** 50 minutes

*As someone who suffers from motion sickness, I use ginger as a natural antiemetic anytime I fly or get on a boat, typically in the form of candied ginger. My frequent consumption of this treat helped me realize its variety of culinary uses in baked goods, salads, and roasted vegetables. Instead of purchasing expensive candied ginger at the store, you can actually make it right in your own kitchen.*

**1 pound ginger, peeled and thinly sliced with a mandoline**

**2 cups sugar, plus more for dusting**

1. Place a wire rack over a baking sheet.

2. Put the ginger in a saucepan, and add just enough water to cover. Bring to a boil over high heat.

3. Reduce the heat to medium. Cover, and cook for about 20 minutes, or until the ginger has softened. Remove from the heat. Reserving ¼ cup of the water, drain.

4. Put the ginger and the reserved ginger water back in the saucepan, and add the sugar. Bring to a boil over high heat, stirring well.

5. Reduce the heat to medium, and cook, stirring occasionally, for 30 to 40 minutes, or until the ginger appears almost dry and the sugar is about to recrystallize. Immediately remove from the heat. Using a slotted spoon, transfer the ginger to the wire rack.

6. Let the ginger dry out for at least 3 hours before dusting it with more sugar to taste.

**NOTE:** If you have a candy thermometer, it should read 225°F when the ginger is ready to be removed from the heat. Candied ginger can be stored in a tightly sealed jar or a zip-top plastic bag at room temperature for up to 4 weeks.

# Green Beans

**Season:** summer, fall

**Flavor profile:** The bright green color of fresh green beans is a good indicator of their slightly sweet, grassy flavor. Their subtle taste makes them a versatile option for side dishes and salads. Plus, they add a delicious crunch to any recipe.

**Pairs with:** red onion, garlic, basil, parsley, thyme, cayenne pepper, paprika, soy sauce, ginger, white beans, almonds, mozzarella and parmesan cheeses

**Varieties:** green beans (a.k.a. string beans), haricots verts (French green beans, thinner), purple string beans, yellow wax beans

**Preparation:** Trim green beans by snapping off the ends with your fingers or using a knife.

**Favorite ways to serve:** blanched, sautéed, roasted

**Nutritional info:** Green beans are low in calories but rich in fiber and micronutrients. They are a good source of immune-boosting vitamin C, providing more than 25 percent of the DV per cup.

**Selection:** Look for green beans that are bright, crisp, and snap easily. They should not have any dark spots or rotting.

**Storage:** Put green beans in a sealed plastic bag or in an airtight container in the refrigerator for up to one week.

# Steamed Green Beans

**SERVES 4** / **PREP TIME:** 10 minutes / **COOK TIME:** 5 to 10 minutes

**1½ pounds green beans, trimmed**
**Soy-Ginger Vinaigrette**
(page 137)

1. Fill a large pot with 2 to 3 inches of water. Place a steamer basket inside the pot, and put the green beans inside the basket. Bring to a boil over high heat. Cover, reduce the heat to medium, and steam for 5 to 7 minutes, or until crisp-tender. Remove from the heat. Transfer to a serving bowl.

2. Add the vinaigrette, and toss until evenly coated.

# Blackened Green Beans

**SERVES 4** / **PREP TIME:** 15 minutes / **COOK TIME:** 10 minutes

*These easy and super flavorful green beans are smothered in blackening seasoning made from a base of paprika, garlic powder, oregano, basil, and cayenne pepper. They're inspired by the delicious blackened green beans on the menu at Grace's Tavern in the Fitler Square neighborhood of Philadelphia, where I first tried this style of green beans several years ago. Serve this easy side dish with almost any entrée for the ultimate flavor boost (and sinus clearing!).*

**4 tablespoons extra-virgin olive oil, divided**

**1 teaspoon smoked paprika**

**½ teaspoon dried oregano**

**½ teaspoon garlic powder**

**½ teaspoon freshly ground black pepper**

**¼ teaspoon salt**

**¼ teaspoon dried basil**

**⅛ teaspoon cayenne pepper**

**1 pound green beans, trimmed**

1. In a large bowl, whisk together 2 tablespoons of olive oil, the paprika, oregano, garlic powder, black pepper, salt, basil, and cayenne pepper.

2. Add the green beans and toss until evenly coated.

3. In a large skillet, warm the remaining 2 tablespoons of olive oil over medium heat.

4. Add the green beans and cook, stirring occasionally, for 5 to 8 minutes, or until tender. Remove from the heat.

**NOTE:** You can also roast the green beans. Line a baking sheet with parchment paper. Arrange the beans in a single layer on the baking sheet, and roast at 400°F for 15 to 20 minutes, or until tender.

# Green Bean and Almond Salad with Balsamic Vinaigrette

**SERVES 4** / **PREP TIME:** 10 minutes / **COOK TIME:** 10 minutes

*Crisp-tender green beans star in this simple side dish made with only five main ingredients. Tangy balsamic vinegar and goat cheese bring out the earthy flavor profile of green beans, while toasted almonds contribute crunch. This dish is light, easy to prepare, and a great option for potlucks, cookouts, or weeknight meals when you're crunched for time.*

**FOR THE SALAD**

1 pound green
  beans, trimmed
½ cup sliced or chopped
  almonds, toasted
¼ cup crumbled
  vegetarian goat cheese

**FOR THE DRESSING**

3 tablespoons extra-virgin
  olive oil
2 tablespoons
  balsamic vinegar
2 teaspoons
  Dijon mustard
Salt

**TO MAKE THE SALAD**

1. Fill a large pot with 2 to 3 inches of water. Place a steamer basket inside the pot, and put the green beans inside the basket. Bring the water to a boil over high heat. Cover, reduce the heat to medium, and cook for 5 to 7 minutes, or until crisp-tender. Remove from the heat. Transfer the green beans to a bowl.

2. Add the almonds and goat cheese. Toss to combine.

**TO MAKE THE DRESSING**

3. In a small bowl, whisk together the olive oil, vinegar, and mustard.

4. Pour the dressing over the salad, and toss until evenly coated. Season with salt to taste.

**NOTE:** Store leftovers in an airtight container in the refrigerator for up to 5 days.

# Cheesy Broiled Green Beans

**SERVES 4** / **PREP TIME:** 10 minutes / **COOK TIME:** 25 minutes

*Tender green beans are blanketed with melted mozzarella and parmesan cheese in this quick side dish. Simple yet drool-worthy, this recipe is a crowd-pleaser that will likely become a favorite of both the kids and adults in your family. It's the kind of dish you'll come back to again and again when you need to put some vegetables on the table on a busy evening, but it's also suitable for holiday meals.*

**1 pound green beans, trimmed**

**1 tablespoon extra-virgin olive oil**

**Salt**

**Freshly ground black pepper**

**1 cup shredded vegetarian mozzarella cheese**

**½ cup freshly grated vegetarian parmesan cheese**

1. Preheat the oven to 400°F. Line a baking sheet with aluminum foil.

2. Arrange the green beans in a single layer on the prepared baking sheet.

3. Drizzle the green beans with the olive oil. Season with salt and pepper.

4. Transfer the baking sheet to the oven, and bake for 15 to 20 minutes, or until the green beans are tender. Remove from the oven.

5. Turn the broiler to high.

6. Push the green beans together on the baking sheet.

7. Sprinkle the mozzarella cheese and parmesan cheese on top.

8. Return the baking sheet to the oven, and broil for 2 to 3 minutes, or until the cheese is bubbly and golden brown. Remove from the oven.

**NOTE:** This dish is best served right away, since leftovers do not keep well in the refrigerator.

# Green Bean Pita Pockets

**SERVES 4** / **PREP TIME:** 15 minutes / **COOK TIME:** 5 minutes

*Quick-cooked green beans dressed in red wine vinegar and dried herbs make these stuffed vegan pita pockets delightfully crunchy. They make for a delicious lunch option that can be prepped in advance and stored in the refrigerator for quick access. I recommend spreading the inside of the pita pocket with a hearty spoonful of the Creamy White Bean Dip, but you can also use the Roasted Carrot and Tahini Dressing (page 77).*

**1 pound green beans, trimmed**

**½ cup thinly sliced red onion**

**3 tablespoons extra-virgin olive oil**

**1 tablespoon red wine vinegar**

**1 teaspoon dried basil**

**Salt**

**4 whole-wheat pitas, halved**

**Creamy White Bean Dip** (page 38)

1. In a large skillet, bring 2 inches of water to a boil over high heat. Fill a bowl with ice water.

2. Add the green beans to the boiling water. Cover, and simmer for 3 minutes, or until crisp-tender. Remove from the heat. Immediately drain, and submerge in the ice water.

3. Drain the green beans again, and put them in a bowl with the onion.

4. Add the olive oil, vinegar, and basil. Season with salt. Toss to coat evenly.

5. Stuff each pita half with the green beans.

6. Add dollops of the white bean dip.

**NOTE:** You can substitute lemon juice for the red wine vinegar. Feel free to add sliced hard-boiled eggs or cheese to bulk up this recipe, but keep in mind that adding eggs or cheese means it will no longer be vegan.

# Herbs

**Season:** spring, summer, fall

**Flavor profile:** Herbs are truly one of the most important groups of seasonings for flavorful, plant-forward cooking. Each herb offers a unique flavor profile, ranging from the cool and sweet taste of fresh mint to the woody, piney notes found in rosemary.

**Pairs with:** dressings, marinades, all vegetables

**Varieties:** rosemary, basil, thyme, oregano, mint, parsley, cilantro, dill, tarragon, sage, chives

**Preparation:** Wash most herbs under running water to clean. Some recipes call for whole leaves, whereas others require chopped herbs.

**Favorite ways to serve:** used as seasonings, mixed into dressings and condiments, dried

**Nutritional info:** Although the exact nutritional benefits of every herb are unclear, it's thought that adding herbs to foods generally has a positive effect on health.

**Selection:** Herbs should have bright-colored leaves that are not wilted or mushy.

**Storage:** Most herbs can be kept for up to one week. Store fresh basil upright in a glass jar with water, covered loosely with a plastic bag at room temperature away from direct sunlight. Rosemary, thyme, and oregano should be kept wrapped in a paper towel inside a plastic bag in the refrigerator. Parsley, cilantro, and mint can be stored upright in glass jars filled with water in the refrigerator. For the best storage results, change the water every two to three days.

# DIY Dried Herbs

**PREP TIME:** at least 1 to 2 weeks to dry

**Herbs of your choice, such as thyme, rosemary, oregano, or sage**

1. If you are harvesting your own herbs, cut them from your garden just before drying.

2. Rinse the herbs under cold running water to clean. Pat dry with paper towels.

3. For each herb, combine 5 to 10 branches together. Tie them together with twine or string, and hang them upside down by the string from a hook, curtain rod, or another platform in a warm room in your home. Some herbs take 1 to 2 weeks to dry, whereas others may take longer. The herbs are properly dried when they look shriveled and brown and feel crunchy when rubbed with your fingers.

**NOTE:** Store dried herbs in small airtight containers for later use.

# Frozen Olive Oil and Rosemary Cubes

**MAKES 12 CUBES** / **PREP TIME:** 5 minutes, plus 4 hours to freeze

*Fresh rosemary is known for its piney flavor and strong fragrance. It pairs wonderfully with fall and winter vegetables, including beets, parsnips, carrots, winter squash, and other root vegetables. If you grow rosemary in your summer garden and want to preserve it for colder months, making frozen olive oil and rosemary cubes is the way to go. You can enjoy the delicious flavors of fresh rosemary all year long with the help of this freezer recipe.*

**1 cup chopped fresh rosemary**

**¾ cup extra-virgin olive oil, plus more as needed**

1. Divide the rosemary equally among the molds in a silicone or plastic ice cube tray.

2. Add enough olive oil to just barely cover the rosemary. Freeze for at least 4 hours.

3. Gently pop the cubes out of the tray, and store in a sealed and labeled zip-top plastic bag in the freezer for later use. When you want to use one, simply add it frozen to the skillet or pot you are using.

**NOTE:** You can use this same method for all kinds of herbs.

# Mint-Tarragon Vinaigrette

**MAKES ABOUT 2 CUPS / PREP TIME:** 10 minutes

*A generally underappreciated herb, tarragon gets its chance to shine alongside sweet mint in this flavorful dressing. If you enjoy licorice flavors, you will love fresh tarragon. Plus, the salty notes from freshly grated parmesan and zesty punch from lemon juice make this herby dressing a full-bodied condiment. It can elevate the flavor of nearly any dish.*

½ cup extra-virgin olive oil

½ cup freshly grated vegetarian parmesan cheese

Juice of 1 lemon

¼ cup chopped fresh tarragon

¼ cup chopped fresh mint

¼ teaspoon salt

1. In a glass jar with a lid, combine the olive oil, parmesan cheese, lemon juice, tarragon, mint, and salt.

2. Seal the lid, and shake well to mix.

**NOTE:** The vinaigrette tastes delicious on shaved, steamed, or roasted asparagus, sautéed peas, salads, and other spring vegetable dishes. Store in the refrigerator for up to two weeks.

# Homemade Chimichurri

**MAKES ABOUT 1 CUP / PREP TIME:** 10 minutes

*Chimichurri is a vibrant green sauce made from fresh parsley and cilantro that's popular in South American cooking. Although it's typically served with meat and fish, it's also a delicious addition to plant-based recipes. You can serve it on top of cauliflower or kohlrabi steaks or use it as a dipping sauce for veggie chips and fries.*

**1 cup loosely packed fresh parsley leaves (about 1 bunch)**

**1 cup loosely packed fresh cilantro leaves (about 1 bunch)**

**4 garlic cloves, minced**

**½ cup extra-virgin olive oil**

**¼ cup red wine vinegar**

**½ teaspoon salt**

**¼ teaspoon freshly ground black pepper**

**¼ teaspoon red pepper flakes**

1. In a food processor, combine the parsley, cilantro, and garlic. Pulse once or twice.

2. Add the olive oil, vinegar, salt, pepper, and red pepper flakes. Pulse until smooth, using a rubber spatula to scrape down the sides as needed.

NOTE: Store in an airtight container in the refrigerator for up to 7 days.

# Herb Compound Butter

**MAKES ABOUT ½ CUP / PREP TIME:** 10 minutes

*As the name suggests, this butter is quite literally compounded with herbs, in addition to freshly squeezed lemon juice. I love making a batch of fresh compound butter to keep in the refrigerator so that I can add a pat to roasted vegetables, vegetable steaks, toast, and biscuits. Melted herb butter can be spread onto thin slices of bread used for bruschetta before toasting them.*

**8 tablespoons (1 stick) unsalted butter, at room temperature**

**2 tablespoons chopped fresh parsley**

**1 tablespoon chopped fresh chives**

**Juice of 1 lemon**

**½ teaspoon salt, plus more as needed**

**¼ teaspoon freshly ground black pepper, plus more as needed**

1. In a medium bowl, using a fork, mix together the butter, parsley, and chives.

2. Add the lemon juice, salt, and pepper. Mix to combine. Season with salt and pepper to taste.

3. Transfer the butter to an airtight container, and store in the refrigerator. Or lay a square of wax paper on a work surface. Spoon the herb butter onto the wax paper. Using a rubber spatula, form it into a log. Wrap up the log, and twist the ends shut. Chill in the refrigerator until you're ready to use, then cut into ¼-inch-thick slices.

**NOTE:** Feel free to swap out the herbs in this recipe with fresh basil, cilantro, tarragon, dill, or oregano. You can roll the butter up in parchment paper or plastic wrap if you don't have wax paper.

# Jicama

**Season:** fall, winter

**Flavor profile:** Native to Mexico, jicama is a type of tuber with brown skin and white flesh that resembles a potato. It has a crunchy texture similar to an apple and a sweet, nutty taste.

**Pairs with:** lime juice, chili powder, cilantro, dill, parsley, red wine vinegar, fresh fruit, soy sauce

**Varieties:** several, but similar in appearance

**Preparation:** Peel jicama with a swivel peeler, then use a knife to cut it into desired shapes.

**Favorite ways to serve:** raw, spiralized, riced, roasted

**Nutritional info:** Jicama packs more than six grams of fiber in just one cup. It is particularly rich in prebiotic fiber that feeds gut bacteria, contributing to a healthy microbiome.

**Selection:** Fresh jicama is firm to the touch and has smooth skin that does not appear dry. Smaller jicama are thought to have a sweeter taste.

**Storage:** Whole jicama can be stored at room temperature in a cool, dry place for up to two weeks or sometimes a little longer. Once it has been peeled and cut, keep it in a sealed plastic bag or airtight container in the refrigerator for up to one week.

# Baked Jicama Fries with Homemade Chimichurri

**SERVES ABOUT 4** / **PREP TIME:** 5 minutes / **COOK TIME:** 35 minutes

**1 large jicama,
    peeled and cut into
    ½-inch-thick strips**
**1 tablespoon extra-virgin
    olive oil**
**½ teaspoon garlic powder**
**Homemade Chimichurri**
    (page 151)**, for dipping**

1. Preheat the oven to 400°F. Line a baking sheet with parchment paper.

2. On the prepared baking sheet, using your hands or a rubber spatula, toss the jicama with the olive oil and garlic powder until evenly coated.

3. Arrange the jicama in a single layer.

4. Transfer the baking sheet to the oven and bake for 30 to 35 minutes, flipping halfway through, or until the jicama is tender and slightly browned.

5. Serve the fries warm with chimichurri or another dipping sauce of choice.

# Chili-Lime Spiralized Jicama Salad

**SERVES 4 / PREP TIME:** 15 minutes

*Raw jicama sticks are commonly served with chili powder, and this recipe showcases that flavor combination in salad form. Jicama's crisp flesh makes it an easy vegetable to spiralize, and the subtle taste lends itself to soaking up the seasonings. This simple side has only three ingredients but is still bursting with flavor, thanks to this all-star headliner of a vegetable.*

**1 medium jicama, peeled and spiralized**

**Juice of 2 limes**

**1 teaspoon chili powder**

**Salt**

1. Using a knife or kitchen scissors, break up any long jicama noodles to make them more manageable.

2. In a large bowl, combine the jicama, lime juice, and chili powder. Season with salt to taste.

**NOTE:** Serve immediately, or store in an airtight container in the refrigerator for up to 5 days.

# Jicama-Mango Salsa

**MAKES ABOUT 6 CUPS / PREP TIME:** 15 minutes

*Or should I say Jica-mango Salsa? This hydrating, juicy snack is the perfect way to cool off on a hot summer's day. It's crunchy, fruity, spicy, and refreshing all at the same time, with simple ingredients to boot. I like eating it with tortilla chips, but I've also found myself enjoying it straight out of the jar with a spoon. You can serve this salsa on grilled vegetable steaks or spooned over roasted zucchini in the summer.*

1 medium jicama, peeled and diced

1 mango, peeled, pitted, and diced

½ cup chopped red onion

1 jalapeño pepper, seeded and finely chopped

2 tablespoons chopped fresh cilantro

2 tablespoons chopped fresh dill

Juice of 1 lime

Salt

1. In a medium bowl, mix together the jicama, mango, onion, jalapeño, cilantro, and dill.

2. Add the lime juice. Season with salt to taste.

3. Chill the salsa for at least 1 hour to allow the flavors to marinate together before serving, or enjoy immediately if you just can't wait.

# Jicama Fried "Rice"

**SERVES 4** / **PREP TIME:** 10 minutes / **COOK TIME:** 15 minutes

*Jicama's crisp texture for the win . . . again. Riced jicama maintains its firmness and does not get mushy, making it an excellent substitution for rice here. You can make this delicious vegetarian main dish with whatever vegetables you have on hand, such as frozen or fresh carrots, broccoli, corn, or peas. Add a couple eggs for some protein and a dash of soy sauce for flavor, and dinner is served.*

**1 medium jicama, peeled and coarsely chopped**

**1 tablespoon extra-virgin olive oil**

**2 teaspoons toasted sesame oil**

**3 to 4 cups vegetables, such as chopped carrots and broccoli, peas, or corn**

**2 large eggs, beaten**

**1 to 2 tablespoons soy sauce**

**2 scallions, green and white parts, thinly sliced**

1. Put the jicama in a food processor, and pulse until it has a rice-like texture.

2. In a large skillet, warm the olive oil and toasted sesame oil over medium heat.

3. Add the vegetables, and cook for 5 to 7 minutes, or until tender.

4. Stir in the jicama, and cook for 3 to 4 minutes, or until warmed through and softened.

5. Push the jicama aside, and pour in the eggs. Wait a minute or two, or until the eggs set, before stirring them into the rest of the fried "rice" with a rubber spatula.

6. Add 1 tablespoon of soy sauce. Taste, and add more as needed. Cook for 1 to 2 minutes, or until the fried rice is heated through. Remove from the heat.

7. Top the fried rice with the scallions, and serve.

**NOTE:** Use tamari in place of soy to make this dish gluten-free. You can add cooked edamame to this dish for more protein. Store leftovers in an airtight container in the refrigerator for up to 3 days.

# Kale and Other Greens

**Season:** spring, fall, winter

**Flavor profile:** Kale is a hearty, leafy green vegetable with a tough texture and earthy taste. Its flavor is stronger than that of spinach and more similar to other greens with robust tastes like collard greens, chard, and beet greens.

**Pairs with:** vinegars, citrus, garlic, olive oil, raisins, dried cranberries, coconut, apples, pecans, walnuts, honey, maple syrup

**Varieties:** Kale can be green or purple in color. The most common varieties are curly kale and lacinato (dinosaur) kale. Other leafy greens include turnip, beet, or mustard greens; collard greens; microgreens; arugula (page 16); bok choy (page 46); chard (page 95); spinach (page 236); and watercress (page 260).

**Preparation:** Use your hands or a knife to remove the leaves from the stems.

Rinse thoroughly under cold running water to clean. Pat dry. To soften kale, massage it in your hands with a drizzle of olive oil.

**Favorite ways to serve:** raw in salads, braised, blended into smoothies

**Nutritional info:** Kale and most other hearty greens are incredibly rich in the antioxidant vitamins A and C. One cup of kale also provides close to 700 percent of the DV of vitamin K, a fat-soluble vitamin that's necessary for proper blood clotting.

**Selection:** Kale and similar leafy green vegetables should have a bright color and be free of dark spots or holes. The leaves should not be wilted or yellow, and the stems should not be dried out.

**Storage:** Store leafy greens unwashed in between paper towels in a sealed plastic bag in the produce drawer of the refrigerator. They typically last for a week, but freshly picked greens may last longer.

# Coconut-Braised Kale

**SERVES 4** / **PREP TIME:** 5 minutes / **COOK TIME:** 10 to 15 minutes

1 (13½-ounce) can full-fat
  coconut milk
1 tablespoon soy sauce
Juice of 1 lime
1 bay leaf
Pinch red pepper flakes
1 bunch kale, stemmed
  and coarsely chopped
Salt

In a large skillet, combine the coconut milk, soy sauce, lime juice, bay leaf, red pepper flakes, and kale. Cook over medium heat, stirring occasionally, for 10 to 12 minutes, or until tender. Remove from the heat. Season with salt to taste.

# Crispy Kale Chips

**SERVES 4** / **PREP TIME:** 10 minutes / **COOK TIME:** 25 minutes

*Satisfy your afternoon cravings with these salty, crispy, and savory kale chips—the perfect snack food. It's easy to "eat your greens" with this recipe, especially when you're not in the mood for a salad. Just remember to follow the directions closely and avoid overcrowding your baking sheets to ensure that the chips get as crispy as possible.*

**1 bunch curly kale,**
**stemmed and**
**coarsely torn**
**1 to 2 tablespoons**
**extra-virgin olive oil**
**1 teaspoon garlic powder**
**Salt**
**Freshly ground**
**black pepper**

1. Preheat the oven to 300°F. Line 2 baking sheets with parchment paper.

2. Pat the kale dry with paper towels. Make sure that the kale is completely dry, since any leftover moisture on the leaves will steam them while cooking and make the chips soggy.

3. Divide the kale equally between the prepared baking sheets.

4. Drizzle the kale with the olive oil (enough to lightly coat the leaves) and use your hands to toss.

5. Arrange the kale in a single layer. Season with the garlic powder, salt, and pepper.

6. Transfer the baking sheets to the oven and bake for 10 minutes.

7. Rotate the baking sheets and bake for 15 minutes, or until the kale is slightly browned and crispy. Remove from the oven.

**NOTE:** Other possible seasoning combinations include 1 teaspoon chili powder with ½ teaspoon paprika and ½ teaspoon garlic powder. For "cheesy" chips, mix 2 tablespoons nutritional yeast with 1 teaspoon garlic powder and salt to taste.

# Massaged Kale, Apple, and Lentil Salad

**SERVES 4 TO 6 / PREP TIME:** 15 minutes

*If you typically shy away from kale because of its tough texture, massaging kale before adding it to dishes may just change your opinion of this leafy green. Work kale with your hands for a few minutes to transform a stubborn green into a tender, more enjoyable vegetable. Trust me, this extra step is well worth it and makes all the difference.*

## FOR THE SALAD

1 bunch kale, stemmed and coarsely torn

1 to 2 teaspoons extra-virgin olive oil

2 Honeycrisp apples, diced

2 cups cooked lentils

1 cup freshly grated vegetarian sharp cheddar cheese

½ cup dried cranberries

## FOR THE DRESSING

½ cup tahini

¼ cup apple cider vinegar

Juice of 1 lemon

2 garlic cloves, minced

Salt

Freshly ground black pepper

## TO MAKE THE SALAD

1. In a large bowl, using your hands, massage the kale with the olive oil for 2 to 3 minutes, or until tender but not mushy.

2. Add the apples, lentils, cheddar cheese, and dried cranberries. Toss to combine.

## TO MAKE THE DRESSING

3. In a small bowl, whisk together the tahini, vinegar, lemon juice, and garlic.

4. Add water, 1 tablespoon at a time (up to ¼ cup total), until the dressing reaches the desired consistency. Season with salt and pepper to taste.

5. Pour the dressing over the salad, and toss until evenly coated.

**NOTE:** This recipe also tastes delicious with the Shallot-Dijon Vinaigrette (page 233). If you are prepping the salad in advance, wait to add the apples and dressing until right before serving to prevent the apples from browning.

# Collard Greens Smoothie

**SERVES 4** / **PREP TIME:** 5 minutes

*Though they're typically associated with Southern cooking, collard greens take on a tropical twist in this refreshing smoothie recipe. With mango, banana, lime, and hints of mint, it's a yummy way to drink your greens for breakfast, after exercise, or as an afternoon snack. These complementary ingredients subdue the subtle bitterness of collard greens and bring out their softer undertones.*

**4 cups coarsely chopped collard greens**

**2 fresh or frozen bananas**

**2 cups fresh or frozen diced mango**

**1 cup full-fat plain Greek yogurt**

**Juice of 1 lime**

**4 to 6 fresh mint leaves, plus more as needed**

1. In a blender, combine the collard greens, bananas, mango, yogurt, lime juice, mint, and 2 cups of water. Blend until smooth. Add more water as needed to reach the desired consistency.

2. Add more mint to taste.

**NOTE:** If you do not use frozen fruit, add a few ice cubes to make the smoothie colder. You can substitute pineapple for the mango and use vanilla yogurt in place of plain for more flavor.

# Sautéed Mustard Greens

**SERVES 4** / **PREP TIME:** 10 minutes / **COOK TIME:** 15 minutes

*When cooked in a skillet with a few simple ingredients, the peppery taste of mustard greens shines. Mustard greens make for a delicious, simple, and interesting side dish next to any entrée and deliver a ton of vitamin K and other nutrients at the same time. Substitute any hearty leafy greens, including turnip, beet, and radish greens, that would otherwise go to waste.*

**1 tablespoon extra-virgin olive oil**

**3 garlic cloves, minced**

**1 bunch mustard greens, chopped**

**Salt**

**Freshly ground black pepper**

**¼ cup vegetable broth**

1. In a large skillet, warm the olive oil over medium heat.

2. Add the garlic, and cook, stirring frequently, for about 1 minute, or until fragrant.

3. Stir in the mustard greens, and cook for 3 to 4 minutes, or until just wilted. Season with salt and pepper.

4. Add the broth, bring to a simmer, and cook for 3 to 4 minutes, or until the greens are tender and some of the broth has cooked off. Remove from the heat. Serve warm.

**NOTE:** For a different flavor profile, add 1 teaspoon toasted sesame oil and a pinch of red pepper flakes to the skillet with the olive oil and garlic.

# Citrusy Microgreens

**SERVES 4** / **PREP TIME:** 5 minutes

*As their name suggests, microgreens are tiny greens that grow from the seeds of vegetables and herbs. Despite their small size, they're rich in nutrients and can be a versatile ingredient. Toss microgreens in freshly squeezed orange and lemon juices for a healthy side salad or garnish. You can even serve this recipe on top of toast with hummus or ricotta for a quick breakfast or lunch.*

**2 tablespoons extra-virgin olive oil**

**1 tablespoon freshly squeezed lemon juice, plus more as needed**

**1 tablespoon freshly squeezed orange juice, plus more as needed**

**2 cups microgreens**

**½ cup salted sunflower seeds**

**Salt**

1. In a bowl, whisk together the olive oil, lemon juice, and orange juice.

2. Add the microgreens and sunflower seeds. Toss until evenly coated. Season with salt. Taste and add more citrus juices as needed.

**NOTE:** The microgreens taste best when enjoyed right away, since they can get soggy after sitting in dressing. Add some orange or lemon zest in addition to the juice for more flavor.

# Kohlrabi

**Season:** spring, fall, winter

**Flavor profile:** Kohlrabi is a bulbous vegetable related to cabbage and turnips. It has stalks with leaves that shoot out of its skin at different areas, but typically only the bulb is eaten. The taste of kohlrabi is very similar to broccoli stems, but older kohlrabi can taste closer to turnips.

**Pairs with:** thyme, rosemary, oregano, chives, dill, basil, tomatoes, lemon, carrots, potatoes, sesame, ginger, butter, mustard

**Varieties:** green, purple

**Preparation:** Remove the stalks, and peel with a swivel peeler or a knife. Use a sharp knife to dice or cut into steaks. Kohlrabi also lends itself very well to being spiralized.

**Favorite ways to serve:** roasted, spiralized, sautéed

**Nutritional info:** Kohlrabi contains a variety of nutrients but is very high in vitamin C. This water-soluble vitamin is necessary for the synthesis of collagen in the body and contributes to wound healing.

**Selection:** Choose kohlrabi that do not have any blemishes or dark spots on the skin. They should feel firm and heavy for their size.

**Storage:** Remove leaves and stalks, wrap in a damp paper towel, and store loosely in a sealed plastic bag. Kohlrabi bulbs should last for about a week in the produce drawer in the refrigerator.

# Roasted Kohlrabi

**SERVES 4 / PREP TIME:** 5 minutes / **COOK TIME:** 35 minutes

1 kohlrabi bulb, peeled
  and diced
1 tablespoon extra-virgin
  olive oil
Salt
Freshly ground
  black pepper

1. Preheat the oven to 450°F. Line a baking sheet with aluminum foil.

2. Spread the kohlrabi out in a single layer on the prepared baking sheet.

3. Drizzle the kohlrabi with the olive oil. Season with salt and pepper.

4. Transfer the baking sheet to the oven, and roast for 30 to 35 minutes, stirring halfway through, or until the kohlrabi is tender and browned. Remove from the oven.

# Kohlrabi Steaks with Herb Compound Butter

**SERVES 4** / **PREP TIME:** 5 minutes / **COOK TIME:** 35 minutes

*Bulbous kohlrabi is easy to cut into ½-inch-thick slices that resemble steak medallions. Roasted kohlrabi steaks also have a mellow, earthy taste, making them a good canvas for flavorful toppings like herb butter. Though these steaks are a fun, plant-based substitution for a carnivorous main dish, it's best to serve them with a higher-protein side dish, like the Cumin-Lime Three Bean Salad (page 36), to make a balanced meal.*

**2 medium kohlrabi bulbs, peeled and cut into ½-inch-thick rounds**

**1 tablespoon extra-virgin olive oil**

**Salt**

**Freshly ground black pepper**

**¼ cup Herb Compound Butter** (page 152)

1. Preheat the oven to 400°F. Line a baking sheet with parchment paper.

2. On the prepared baking sheet, brush each side of the kohlrabi with the olive oil. Season with salt and pepper.

3. Arrange the kohlrabi in a single layer.

4. Transfer the baking sheet to the oven and bake for 30 to 35 minutes, flipping halfway through, or until the kohlrabi is tender. Remove from the oven.

5. Serve the kohlrabi steaks warm with the herb butter.

# Kohlrabi Noodles with Red Sauce and Kidney Beans

**SERVES 4** / **PREP TIME:** 15 minutes / **COOK TIME:** 15 to 20 minutes

*Kohlrabi noodles hold up especially well in cooking and even resemble regular noodles. They capture the delicious flavor of marinara and mimic the perfect texture of al dente spaghetti. The addition of kidney beans packs some more protein and fiber into the dish, rounding it out nutritionally and making it a quick vegetarian main for busy evenings.*

**2 tablespoons extra-virgin olive oil**

**½ yellow onion, diced**

**3 garlic cloves, minced**

**3 kohlrabi bulbs, trimmed and spiralized**

**2 cups Homemade Tomato Sauce** (page 251)

**½ teaspoon dried oregano**

**½ teaspoon dried basil**

**⅛ teaspoon red pepper flakes** (optional)

**Salt**

**1 (15-ounce) can red kidney beans, drained and rinsed**

1. In a large skillet, warm the olive oil over medium heat.

2. Add the onion and garlic. Cook for 3 to 4 minutes, or until fragrant.

3. Add the kohlrabi, and cook, stirring frequently, for 5 to 7 minutes, or until softened.

4. Add the tomato sauce, oregano, basil, and red pepper flakes (if using). Season with salt.

5. Reduce the heat to low. Simmer for 5 to 7 minutes, or until warmed through. Remove from the heat.

6. Mix in the beans, and serve warm.

NOTE: This meal tastes delicious with freshly grated vegetarian Parmesan cheese and a side of crunchy garlic bread.

# Leeks

**Season:** winter

**Flavor profile:** Leeks taste similar to their relatives—onions, shallots, scallions, and garlic. However, their flavor is milder and not as zesty compared to other types of alliums. Raw leeks have a crunchy texture, whereas cooked leeks are tender and buttery. Although all parts of a leek are edible, most recipes use only the white and light green parts.

**Pairs with:** potatoes, cheese, cream, garlic, thyme, rosemary, white cooking wine

**Varieties:** light green, less hardy leaves; blue-green, hardier leaves

**Preparation:** Cut off the bottoms and dark green leaves on top, leaving just the white and light green parts of the leek. Cut in half, and rinse under cold running water. Use your fingers to gently open the layers as you rinse to ensure that you remove all of the dirt.

**Favorite ways to serve:** roasted, braised, sautéed

**Nutritional info:** Leeks contain several of the same beneficial compounds as onions and garlic, including thiosulfinates that may help reduce blood pressure and boost heart health, among other benefits.

**Selection:** To get the most out of leeks, choose ones that have long white and green stalks. The leaves should be firm with a deep green color free of yellow spots.

**Storage:** You can keep leeks in a sealed bag or wrapped in plastic wrap in the vegetable drawer of the refrigerator. Use within 10 days.

# Roasted Leeks

**SERVES 4** / **PREP TIME:** 10 minutes / **COOK TIME:** 20 minutes

8 leeks, white and light
   green parts, halved
1 tablespoon extra-virgin
   olive oil
Salt
Freshly ground
   black pepper

1. Preheat the oven to 400°F. Line a baking sheet with parchment paper.

2. Brush each side of the leeks with the olive oil. Season with salt and pepper.

3. Arrange the leeks, cut-side down, on the prepared baking sheet.

4. Transfer the baking sheet to the oven and roast for 20 minutes, flipping halfway through, or until the leeks are slightly browned and tender. Remove from the oven.

**NOTE:** For more flavor, season the leeks with garlic powder before roasting.

# Garlicky Leeks with Brie on Crostini

**SERVES 6** / **PREP TIME:** 15 minutes / **COOK TIME:** 15 minutes

*This simply elegant appetizer features the delightful taste of cooked leeks alongside crunchy bread and creamy brie. Each crostini has a variety of textures and packs a ton of flavor in just a few bites. Put out a tray of this tasty snack for your next dinner party or holiday meal, and watch your guests snatch them up in minutes.*

1 baguette, cut into ½-inch-thick slices

3 tablespoons extra-virgin olive oil, divided

4 garlic cloves, minced

3 leeks, white and light green parts, halved and thinly sliced

1 tablespoon fresh thyme leaves, plus more for garnish (optional)

Salt

Freshly ground black pepper

8 ounces brie, cut into ¼-inch-thick pieces

1. Preheat the oven to 350°F. Line a baking sheet with parchment paper.

2. On the prepared baking sheet, brush both sides of the baguette slices with 1 tablespoon of olive oil.

3. Transfer the baking sheet to the oven and bake for 10 to 14 minutes, flipping baguette slices halfway through, or until golden. Remove from the oven. Let cool.

4. Meanwhile, in a large skillet, warm the remaining 2 tablespoons of olive oil over medium heat.

5. Add the garlic, and cook for 1 to 2 minutes, or until fragrant.

6. Add the leeks and thyme. Cook for 8 to 10 minutes, or until the leeks are tender. Season with salt and pepper. Remove from the heat.

7. Place a slice of brie on each piece of toasted baguette. Spoon the leek mixture on top.

8. Garnish with more thyme (if using).

**NOTE:** You can serve the leeks cold or warm. The leek mixture can be made up to a day in advance. Store in an airtight container in the refrigerator. Assemble the crostini just before serving.

# Lettuce

**Season:** spring, fall

**Flavor profile:** Fresh lettuce has a light, hydrating taste and crisp texture. Some varieties have a stronger flavor than others, but in general, lettuce is mild and vegetal with a high water content. Dressings and other toppings can completely transform the flavor profile of lettuce.

**Pairs with:** vinaigrettes, creamy dressings, cheese, crunchy vegetables like carrots and radishes, fresh and dried fruit

**Varieties:** romaine, butter (a.k.a. Bibb or Boston), green or red leaf, iceberg

**Preparation:** Cut a head of lettuce in half, remove the core and ends, and separate the leaves. Wash under running water in a colander. Pat dry, or use a salad spinner to remove excess water.

**Favorite ways to serve:** raw in salads, stuffed, seared, grilled

**Nutritional info:** Since lettuce is mostly made of water, it's very low in calories but still packs several vitamins and minerals. Depending on the variety, lettuce may provide calcium, folate, phosphorus, and vitamins A, C, and K.

**Selection:** Choose heads of lettuce that have crisp leaves with no signs of wilting. The leaves should be intact, and iceberg lettuce in particular should be tightly packed.

**Storage:** Prepared and washed lettuce should be stored in between paper towels in a plastic bag in the refrigerator for up to 1 week. Heads of lettuce can be loosely wrapped in paper towels and kept in the produce drawer for 10 days.

# Grilled Romaine Lettuce

**SERVES 4** / **PREP TIME:** 5 minutes / **COOK TIME:** 5 minutes

**4 romaine hearts**

**2 tablespoons extra-virgin olive oil**

**1 tablespoon apple cider vinegar**

**1 teaspoon garlic powder**

**¼ teaspoon salt**

**Freshly ground black pepper**

1. Preheat the grill on medium-high heat.

2. Cut about 2 inches off the top of each head of romaine, and shave off the very bottom of the root, leaving the rest of the root intact.

3. In a small bowl, whisk together the olive oil, vinegar, garlic powder, and salt. Season with pepper.

4. Brush the mixture over all sides of the romaine.

5. Put the romaine directly on the grill or on a vegetable mat on the grill. Cook, turning with tongs for even cooking, for 1 to 2 minutes on each side, or until slightly charred. Remove from the heat.

# Blueberry and Butter Lettuce Salad with Poppy Seed Dressing

**SERVES 4 / PREP TIME:** 15 minutes

*With crisp butter lettuce and fresh blueberries, this salad is a perfect dish for spring and early summer. It's colorful, refreshing, and light, and has just the right amount of tart goat cheese to complement the sweet poppy seed dressing that ties the whole salad together. Add your favorite nut or seed, like pecans, sunflower seeds, or walnuts for a little more oomph, or serve it as is on the side with veggie burgers.*

### FOR THE DRESSING

¼ cup canola oil

2 tablespoons white
   wine vinegar

2 tablespoons honey

1 teaspoon poppy seeds

½ teaspoon dried mustard

¼ teaspoon salt

### FOR THE SALAD

1 head butter lettuce,
   coarsely torn

2 cups fresh blueberries

½ cup diced red onion

½ cup crumbled
   vegetarian goat cheese

### TO MAKE THE DRESSING

1. In a large bowl, mix together the canola oil, vinegar, honey, poppy seeds, dried mustard, and salt.

### TO MAKE THE SALAD

2. Add the lettuce, blueberries, onion, and goat cheese. Toss together until evenly coated.

**NOTE:** You can substitute red wine vinegar, Champagne vinegar, or white balsamic vinegar for the white wine vinegar. To make this dish vegan, use maple syrup instead of honey, and omit the cheese.

# Lettuce Cups with Quick Egg Salad

**SERVES 6 / PREP TIME:** 15 minutes

*Whole lettuce leaves make great vehicles for protein-rich salads. Instead of serving egg salad on bread, this recipe uses lettuce cups to add a refreshing crunch and some bonus fiber, vitamins, and minerals. Separate, wash, and dry the lettuce leaves and make the egg salad in advance to have a quick option for lunch or dinner or whenever you need it. Any type of lettuce—butter, romaine, leaf, or iceberg—works in this recipe.*

**8 hard-boiled eggs,
   peeled and chopped**

**2 celery stalks,
   thinly sliced**

**½ cup full-fat plain
   Greek yogurt**

**1 tablespoon
   Dijon mustard**

**Salt**

**Freshly ground
   black pepper**

**Chopped fresh dill or
   chives** (optional)

**1 head lettuce,
   leaves separated**

1. In a medium bowl, mix together the eggs and celery.

2. In a measuring cup, mix together the yogurt and mustard. Pour over the egg mixture.

3. Using a fork, gently smash the eggs, and mix together the salad. Season with salt and pepper to taste.

4. Add dill (if using).

5. Spoon the egg salad onto the lettuce leaves.

**NOTE:** To make hard-boiled eggs, put them in a saucepan with 1 inch of water. Cover, bring to a boil over high heat, and cook for 5 to 7 minutes. Transfer to a bowl filled with cold water, and let sit for a few minutes. Drain and peel. Other possible additions to this salad include red onion, lemon juice, paprika, relish, or a chopped refrigerator pickle (see page 111).

# Wedge Salad with Greek Yogurt and Blue Cheese Dressing

**SERVES 4 / PREP TIME:** 10 minutes

*A classic item on pub menus, wedge salad is typically made with large chunks of iceberg lettuce, bacon bits, cherry tomatoes, and creamy blue cheese dressing. This lightened up version features many of the same ingredients but with a yogurt-based dressing and the addition of crispy chickpeas. It can be served as a vegetarian main dish or on the side with the Black-and-Blue-Style Portabella Burgers (page 183).*

**FOR THE DRESSING**

½ cup full-fat plain
Greek yogurt
¼ cup crumbled
vegetarian blue cheese
1 tablespoon white
wine vinegar
1 teaspoon garlic powder
Salt
Freshly ground
black pepper

**FOR THE SALAD**

1 head iceberg
lettuce, quartered
1 cup cherry
tomatoes, halved
½ cup diced red onion
¼ cup crumbled
vegetarian blue cheese
Paprika-Roasted
Chickpeas (page 37)
2 tablespoons chopped
fresh chives

**TO MAKE THE DRESSING**

1. In a small bowl, whisk together the yogurt, blue cheese, vinegar, and garlic powder. Season with salt and pepper to taste. Add a dash of water as needed to reach the desired consistency.

**TO MAKE THE SALAD**

2. Put a wedge of lettuce on each of 4 plates.

3. Divide the tomatoes, onion, blue cheese, chickpeas, and chives equally over the wedges.

4. Drizzle the dressing over the salads, and enjoy immediately.

**NOTE:** You can prepare the dressing up to 5 days in advance and store in an airtight container until you're ready to serve the salad.

# Mushrooms

**Season:** spring, fall

**Flavor profile:** With a rich umami flavor and meaty texture, mushrooms are a common substitution for meat in vegetarian meals. Though they are technically a type of fungi, mushrooms are treated similarly to vegetables in the kitchen. Raw mushrooms have a mild, earthy taste, whereas cooked mushrooms soak up flavors like a sponge.

**Pairs with:** garlic, onions, lemon, balsamic vinegar, soy sauce, sesame oil, paprika, rosemary, thyme, oregano

**Varieties:** portabella, cremini, oyster, shiitake, white button, chanterelle, porcini

**Preparation:** Brush mushrooms with a damp paper towel to remove dirt. Use a knife to quarter or thinly slice, with or without the stems intact.

**Favorite ways to serve:** sautéed, grilled, stuffed

**Nutritional info:** Mushrooms are a good source of water-soluble B vitamins, including niacin, riboflavin, thiamin, and pantothenic acid. B vitamins help the body metabolize food and extract energy from proteins, fats, and carbohydrates.

**Selection:** Mushrooms should be firm to the touch with a uniform color, and the caps should show no signs of shriveling. Avoid mushrooms that are slimy or appear dried out.

**Storage:** Put mushrooms in a brown paper bag, fold the top, and refrigerate. You can also keep them in their original packaging or a sealed container. Mushrooms last for at least one week.

# Balsamic-Roasted Mushrooms

**SERVES 4** / **PREP TIME:** 10 minutes / **COOK TIME:** 25 minutes

2 tablespoons extra-virgin olive oil

1 tablespoon balsamic vinegar

1 tablespoon fresh thyme leaves

1 teaspoon garlic powder

1 pound cremini mushrooms, quartered

Salt

1. Preheat the oven to 400°F. Line a baking sheet with parchment paper.

2. In a medium bowl, whisk together the olive oil, vinegar, thyme, and garlic powder.

3. Add the mushrooms, and mix until coated.

4. Spread the mushrooms out in a single layer on the prepared baking sheet. Season with salt.

5. Transfer the baking sheet to the oven, and roast for 20 to 25 minutes, or until the mushrooms are tender. Remove from the oven.

# Spinach and White Bean Stir-Fry Stuffed Mushrooms

**SERVES 4** / **PREP TIME:** 5 minutes / **COOK TIME:** 20 minutes

*The shape of portabella mushroom caps makes them perfect for stuffing. For this easy recipe, whip up the stir-fry on the stove while the caps roast in the oven. Stuff the portabellas with it, and dinner is served. This simple twist transforms an already delicious dish into a tasty combination that now showcases the meaty texture and savory flavor of mushrooms.*

**8 portabella mushrooms caps, stemmed**

**1 tablespoon extra-virgin olive oil**

**Salt**

**Freshly ground black pepper**

**Spinach and White Bean Stir-Fry** (page 239)

1. Preheat the oven to 400°F. Line a baking sheet with parchment paper.

2. On the prepared baking sheet, brush each side of the mushroom caps with the olive oil.

3. Arrange the mushrooms in a single layer. Season with salt and pepper.

4. Transfer the baking sheet to the oven and roast for about 20 minutes, flipping halfway through, or until the mushrooms are tender. Remove from the oven.

5. Spoon the stir-fry into the mushrooms and serve warm.

**NOTE:** These are best enjoyed right away, since they do not keep well in the refrigerator.

# Mushroom Chorizo Quesadillas

**SERVES 6** / **PREP TIME:** 10 minutes / **COOK TIME:** 45 minutes

*In this recipe, finely chopped mushrooms are combined with rich walnuts and typical chorizo spices for a vegetarian take on ground sausage. The texture is reminiscent of the real deal, and the taste is just as delicious. Making quesadillas is one of the best ways to enjoy mushroom chorizo, but you can also stuff it into tacos and burritos or mix it into a breakfast hash.*

**8 ounces cremini mushrooms, halved**

**1 cup walnuts**

**4 garlic cloves, minced**

**2 teaspoons ground cumin**

**1 teaspoon smoked paprika**

**1 teaspoon dried oregano**

**1 tablespoon extra-virgin olive oil**

**Salt**

**Freshly ground black pepper**

**6 flour tortillas**

**1½ cups shredded vegetarian Mexican cheese**

1. In a food processor, combine the mushrooms, walnuts, garlic, cumin, paprika, and oregano. Pulse, stopping to scrape down the sides as needed, until the ingredients are ground into a meat-like texture.

2. In a large skillet, warm the olive oil over medium heat.

3. Add the mushroom chorizo and cook, stirring, for 12 to 15 minutes, or until most of the moisture from the mushrooms has dried up. Season with salt and pepper. Transfer to a bowl.

4. Put a tortilla in the skillet and sprinkle one half with the Mexican cheese. Spoon some mushroom chorizo on top, and add another layer of cheese. Cover, and cook for about 2 minutes, or until the cheese starts to melt.

5. Fold the other half of the tortilla over the stuffing, and cook for 2 to 3 minutes, or until the cheese has fully melted. Transfer to a plate. Repeat with the remaining tortillas. Remove from the heat.

**NOTE:** You can make the mushroom chorizo in advance and store in an airtight container in the refrigerator until you're ready to cook the quesadillas. Serve with sour cream, Avocado-Lime Mash (page 29), or Arugula Salsa Verde (page 18) as desired.

# Mushroom Chips

**SERVES 4** / **PREP TIME:** 10 minutes / **COOK TIME:** 50 minutes

*If you love the umami taste of mushrooms, this one is for you. The 'shrooms are thinly sliced and slow-roasted, making them highly concentrated with flavor. Mushroom chips are so potently delicious that you'll only need a handful to satisfy your snack craving. You can also enjoy them on salads, a charcuterie board, or crackers spread with cream cheese.*

**2 portabella mushrooms**

**2 tablespoons extra-virgin olive oil, plus more as needed**

**Salt**

**Freshly ground black pepper**

1. Preheat the oven to 300°F. Line a baking sheet with parchment paper.

2. Carefully remove the stems of the mushrooms without tearing the caps. It's also helpful to peel the top layer of skin off the caps so they don't get stuck in the mandoline. Slice the mushrooms with a mandoline, or use a sharp knife to cut them into ⅛-inch-thick slices.

3. On the prepared baking sheet, brush each side of the mushrooms with the olive oil. Season with salt and pepper.

4. Arrange the mushrooms in a single layer.

5. Transfer the baking sheet to the oven and bake for 45 to 50 minutes, or until the mushrooms are completely dry and crispy with a dark color. Remove from the oven. Let cool for a few minutes before eating.

**NOTE:** Make sure the mushrooms are crispy before taking them out of the oven, because they will not crisp up like other veggie chips at room temperature. Store in an airtight container at room temperature for up to 1 week.

# Black-and-Blue-Style Portabella Burgers

**SERVES 4** / **PREP TIME:** 10 minutes / **COOK TIME:** 5 to 10 minutes

*Portabella mushrooms shine in this plant-based twist on black-and-blue burgers, which are typically made with blue cheese and mildly spicy blackening seasoning that's similar to Cajun and Creole spice blends. The mushrooms' spongy texture soaks up every last bit of the blackening seasoning (the same one used on the Blackened Green Beans on page 143), and their caps serve as a perfect vehicle for melted blue cheese. These "burgers" are a delicious, easy, and quick option for cookouts and summer parties.*

2 tablespoons extra-virgin olive oil

1 teaspoon smoked paprika

½ teaspoon dried oregano

½ teaspoon garlic powder

½ teaspoon freshly ground black pepper

¼ teaspoon salt

¼ teaspoon dried basil

⅛ teaspoon cayenne pepper

4 portabella mushroom caps, stemmed

½ cup crumbled vegetarian blue cheese

1. Preheat the grill on medium-high heat.

2. In a small bowl, whisk together the olive oil, paprika, oregano, garlic powder, black pepper, salt, basil, and cayenne pepper.

3. Brush each side of the mushroom caps with the blackening seasoning.

4. Place the mushrooms, gill-side down, on the grill. Cover and cook for 3 to 4 minutes, or until tender and slightly charred.

5. Flip the mushrooms over. Fill the centers with the blue cheese. Cover and cook for 3 to 4 minutes, or until the cheese has melted. Remove from the heat. Enjoy warm.

**NOTE:** Eat these burgers with a fork and knife or stuffed into a toasted bun. You can also top them with the Shallot Marmalade (page 235). If you don't have a grill, use a grill pan. When it's time to melt the cheese, cover the burgers with a skillet lid to keep the heat in.

# Mushroom and Lentil Gravy

**SERVES 4** / **PREP TIME:** 5 minutes / **COOK TIME:** 25 minutes

*Savory mushroom gravy is the ultimate comfort food, and the addition of lentils makes it a suitable source of protein to serve over roasted or mashed vegetables. You can thicken it with cornstarch to mimic traditional gravy or skip that step to serve it like a stew. I like to make this recipe for a cozy meal on a cold evening, but it also tastes delicious served over buttermilk biscuits for breakfast.*

**1 tablespoon extra-virgin olive oil**

**8 ounces cremini mushrooms, chopped**

**1 small yellow onion, diced**

**½ teaspoon dried thyme**

**½ teaspoon dried rosemary**

**½ cup green lentils**

**2 cups vegetable broth**

**Salt**

**1 tablespoon cornstarch** (optional)

1. In a large saucepan, warm the olive oil over medium heat.

2. Add the mushrooms and onion. Cook for 5 to 7 minutes, or until tender.

3. Stir in the thyme, rosemary, lentils, and broth. Season with salt.

4. Increase the heat to medium-high and bring to a boil.

5. Reduce the heat to medium-low. Simmer, uncovered, for 12 to 15 minutes, or until the lentils are tender.

6. If you want to thicken the gravy, in a small bowl, whisk together the cornstarch and 2 tablespoons of water. Add the mixture to the gravy, and cook, stirring constantly, for about 1 minute, or until beginning to thicken. Remove from the heat. Serve warm.

**NOTE:** Store leftovers in an airtight container in the refrigerator for up to 4 days. Reheat in a saucepan over medium-low heat, stirring frequently to prevent scorching.

# Onions

**Season:** spring, fall, winter

**Flavor profile:** Depending on the type, the taste of onions ranges from strong and zesty to sweet and mild. They are one of the most versatile and widely used foods, adding base flavor to soups, stir-fries, sauces, and more.

**Pairs with:** garlic, carrots, celery, butter, olive oil, cream or milk, black pepper, thyme, balsamic vinegar

**Varieties:** yellow, sweet, white, red, green (scallions), shallots (page 231)

**Preparation:** Trim the top, and peel off the papery skin with your fingers. To dice an onion, cut it in half from the root end to the top. Then in each half, make vertical cuts ½-inch apart from the root end to the top, followed by perpendicular cuts across. Remove and discard the ends after dicing.

**Favorite ways to serve:** sautéed, roasted, caramelized, pickled

**Nutritional info:** Onions provide vitamin C, potassium, and several antioxidant compounds. They are also rich in prebiotic fibers called fructans that feed gut bacteria.

**Selection:** Fresh onions are firm and heavy with dry skins and tight necks. Old or rotten onions feel soft or mushy.

**Storage:** Onions can be stored for up to four weeks in a cool, dry spot in the kitchen.

# Stuffed Roasted Onions

**SERVES 4** / **PREP TIME:** 10 minutes / **COOK TIME:** 50 to 55 minutes

*If you love the flavor of onions, get ready to fall head over heels for their creamy texture with this recipe. Whole roasted onions are a culinary treat that showcase just how special they can be as the mainstay of a meal. Although you can enjoy them plain as a side dish, they taste even more delicious with a breaded zucchini stuffing and layer of melted cheese.*

## FOR THE ONIONS

4 sweet onions, peeled
2 tablespoons extra-virgin olive oil
2 tablespoons balsamic vinegar
4 tablespoons (½ stick) salted butter
¼ teaspoon salt

## FOR THE STUFFING

1 tablespoon extra-virgin olive oil
2 cups diced zucchini
3 garlic cloves, minced
¼ cup bread crumbs
½ cup shredded vegetarian mozzarella cheese

## TO MAKE THE ONIONS

1. Preheat the oven to 400°F. Line an 8-by-8-inch baking dish with aluminum foil.

2. Cut about ¼ inch off the tops and bottoms of the onions so that they sit flat in the dish. Place in the prepared baking dish.

3. In a small bowl, whisk together the olive oil and vinegar.

4. Drizzle the mixture over the onions and place 1 tablespoon of butter on each onion. Season with the salt.

5. Transfer the baking dish to the oven and roast for about 50 minutes, or until the onions are tender. Remove from the oven.

## TO MAKE THE STUFFING

6. About 10 minutes before the onions are finished roasting, in a skillet, warm the olive oil over medium heat.

7. Add the zucchini and garlic. Cook for 7 to 10 minutes, or until tender. Remove from the heat.

8. Add the bread crumbs, and mix until the zucchini are coated.

9.  When the onions are finished cooking, scoop out some of the flesh inside to make room for the stuffing. Mix it into the zucchini mixture, if desired. Spoon the stuffing into each onion.

10. Sprinkle the mozzarella cheese on top.

11. Set the oven to broil.

12. Return the baking dish to the oven on the highest rack and broil for 1 to 2 minutes, or until the cheese has melted. Remove from the oven.

NOTE: Don't skip lining the baking dish, since onion juices can stain dishes and are difficult to clean.

# Scallion Pancakes

**MAKES 4 PANCAKES / PREP TIME:** 40 minutes / **COOK TIME:** 15 to 25 minutes

*Savory scallion pancakes, made from a basic dough speckled with sliced scallions, are one of my favorite foods to order at Chinese restaurants. After years of enjoying them during dinners out, I was pleased to discover that they are incredibly easy to make at home. These crispy pancakes are a great way to use up leftover scallions, but they're delicious enough to warrant a trip to the store just to get some for this recipe, too.*

## FOR THE PANCAKES

**2 cups all-purpose flour, plus more for dusting**

**½ teaspoon salt**

**½ teaspoon garlic powder**

**¾ cup just-boiling water, plus 1 to 2 tablespoons as needed**

**¼ cup canola oil, plus more for cooking**

**3 scallions, green and white parts, thinly sliced**

## FOR THE DIPPING SAUCE

**2 tablespoons soy sauce**

**1 scallion, green and white parts, thinly sliced**

**1 tablespoon rice vinegar**

**1 teaspoon sesame oil**

**1 teaspoon Garlic-Infused Honey** (page 134) **or plain honey**

## TO MAKE THE PANCAKES

1. In a large bowl, mix together the flour, salt, and garlic powder.

2. Pour in the water, and stir until the dough comes together.

3. Using your hands, knead the dough for 2 minutes. If it's not sticking together, add the remaining 1 to 2 tablespoons of just-boiling water. The dough should be moist but not overly sticky.

4. Shape the dough into a ball and cover the bowl with plastic wrap. Let sit for 20 minutes.

5. Dust a clean, dry work surface with flour.

6. Cut the dough into 4 pieces and shape into small balls.

7. Using a rolling pin, roll out each dough ball into an 8-inch circle.

8. Brush the surface of each circle with the oil, and sprinkle the scallion on top.

CONTINUED

9. Roll up one circle to make a log. Then take the right side of the log, and curl it toward the center. The dough should look like a snail's shell at this point. Flatten the dough with your hand, then roll it out again into a thin circle. Some scallions may pop out during this process, which is normal. Repeat for the other dough circles.

10. In a skillet, warm a small amount of canola oil over medium heat.

11. One at a time, add the pancakes and cook for 2 to 3 minutes on each side, or until golden brown. Add more oil to the skillet in between pancakes as needed. Remove from the heat.

**TO MAKE THE DIPPING SAUCE**

12. In a small bowl, whisk together the soy sauce, scallion, vinegar, sesame oil, and Garlic-Infused Honey.

13. Serve the pancakes warm, cut into triangles, with the sauce on the side.

# Make-Ahead Caramelized Onions

**SERVES 4 / PREP TIME:** 5 minutes / **COOK TIME:** 50 minutes

**2 tablespoons salted butter or extra-virgin olive oil**

**2 onions, thinly sliced**

**½ teaspoon salt, plus more as needed**

1. In a large skillet, melt the butter over medium heat.

2. Add the onions and salt. Stir until evenly coated.

3. Reduce the heat to medium-low. Cook, stirring every few minutes, for 40 to 50 minutes, or until the onions are caramelized and tender. If the onions start to stick, pour in a splash of water to deglaze the skillet and scrape up the brown bits. Remove from the heat.

NOTE: Store the onions in an airtight container in the refrigerator for up to 1 week, and add to recipes as desired. You can also freeze them in a zip-top plastic bag or in smaller portions in an ice cube tray covered with a plastic bag for up to 3 months.

# Quick Pickled Red Onions

**MAKES 2 (8-OUNCE) JARS** / **PREP TIME:** 10 minutes / **COOK TIME:** 5 minutes

*Pickled red onions are my favorite vegetable-based condiment. They add a yummy crunch and burst of sweet, tangy flavor to tacos, sandwiches, nachos, cheese boards, avocado toast, and more. They disappear pretty quickly in our household. But luckily, this recipe takes almost no time to prepare and uses basic pantry ingredients, so I can whip up a batch every week if needed.*

**1 red onion, thinly sliced**

**½ cup apple cider vinegar**

**1 tablespoon granulated sugar**

**1 teaspoon salt**

1. Divide the onion equally between 2 (8-ounce) jars, or use 1 (16-ounce) jar.

2. In a small saucepan, bring the vinegar, sugar, salt, and ½ cup of water to a simmer over medium heat, stirring until the sugar dissolves. Remove from the heat.

3. Pour the brine equally over the onions.

4. Seal the jars, and let the onions sit for 30 minutes at room temperature.

5. Transfer the jars to the refrigerator.

**NOTE:** The pickled onions will last for up to three weeks in the refrigerator. You can substitute white wine vinegar or red wine vinegar for the apple cider vinegar. For some added flavor, mix in 2 teaspoons whole peppercorns, fennel seeds, or caraway seeds. See Avocado Toast with Quick Pickled Red Onions (page 32) for a tasty way to use these onions.

# Scallion and Pea Orzo Fried "Rice"

**SERVES 4 TO 6** / **PREP TIME:** 10 minutes / **COOK TIME:** 15 minutes

*Transform a single bunch of scallions into a healthy and delicious meal with this easy fried "rice." With a similar shape and size to rice, orzo is a fun substitution to mix things up in the grain department. This dish comes together quickly, making it an ideal option for busy nights when you're hankering for something filling and nutritious.*

**1 tablespoon extra-virgin olive oil**

**1 bunch scallions, green and white parts, thinly sliced**

**2 cups green peas**

**½ cup soy sauce**

**2½ cups cooked orzo pasta**

**4 large eggs, beaten**

**½ cup chopped cashews**

1. In a large skillet, warm the olive oil over medium heat.

2. Stir in the scallions and peas. Cook for 3 to 5 minutes, or until beginning to soften.

3. Add the soy sauce and pasta. Cook for 3 to 4 minutes, or until thoroughly combined and the vegetables are tender.

4. Using a spoon, push the vegetables to one side of the skillet.

5. Add the eggs and cook for a couple minutes, or until they set on the bottom, before mixing them into the rest of the stir-fry. Cook for 1 to 2 minutes, or until warmed through. Remove from the heat.

6. Sprinkle the fried rice with the cashews.

**NOTE:** If you don't have fresh peas, use frozen. They do not need to be thawed and can be added directly to the skillet with the scallions.

# Parsnips

**Season:** fall, winter

**Flavor profile:** Although they look like pale carrots, parsnips have a distinct flavor that's brought out by roasting: sweet and nutty with hints of licorice. They're also starchier than carrots and have a creamy consistency when cooked.

**Pairs with:** olive oil, butter, cinnamon, nutmeg, raisins, maple syrup, honey, apples, sage, garlic, pears, carrots, potatoes

**Varieties:** several that range in color from off-white to light yellow

**Preparation:** Scrub clean with a vegetable brush, and remove skin with a swivel peeler, if desired. Slice or dice with a sharp knife.

**Favorite ways to serve:** roasted, shaved, shredded, mashed

**Nutritional info:** Parsnips provide several micronutrients and are a good source of vitamin C, which helps protect cells from free-radical damage associated with disease development.

**Selection:** Look for parsnips that are firm and unblemished. They should not feel soft or appear shriveled.

**Storage:** Keep parsnips in a sealed plastic bag in the crisper drawer. If the greens are attached, cut them off one inch from the roots before storing. They can be stored for up to two weeks.

# Thyme-Roasted Parsnip Coins

**SERVES 4** / **PREP TIME:** 10 minutes / **COOK TIME:** 35 minutes

**6 parsnips, cut into ½-inch-thick coins**

**2 tablespoons extra-virgin olive oil**

**1 teaspoon dried thyme or 1 tablespoon fresh**

**Salt**

1. Preheat the oven to 400°F. Line a baking sheet with parchment paper.

2. In a large bowl, toss the parsnips with the olive oil and thyme until evenly coated.

3. Arrange the parsnips in a single layer on the prepared baking sheet. Season with salt.

4. Transfer the baking sheet to the oven and roast for 25 to 35 minutes, stirring halfway through, or until the parsnips are tender and browned. Remove from the oven.

# Shaved Parsnips with Dates and Sage Vinaigrette

**SERVES 4 / PREP TIME:** 15 minutes

*It's hard to believe that such an elegant dish takes only 15 minutes to prepare. Thanks to a beautiful marriage of fall flavors, this simple salad deserves a place at your holiday table. The sweet and slightly nutty taste of raw parsnips is an exquisite match for the caramel undertones of fresh dates. These ingredients shine under a sage-based dressing with a touch of maple syrup.*

**FOR THE SAGE VINAIGRETTE**

3 tablespoons extra-virgin olive oil

1 tablespoon maple syrup

1 tablespoon apple cider vinegar

1 tablespoon chopped fresh sage

**FOR THE SALAD**

3 parsnips, peeled and shaved into thin strips

6 to 8 dates, pitted and thinly sliced

**TO MAKE THE SAGE VINAIGRETTE**

1.  In a large bowl, whisk together the olive oil, maple syrup, vinegar, and sage.

**TO MAKE THE SALAD**

2.  Add the parsnips and dates. Toss until evenly coated. Serve immediately.

**NOTE:** The few ingredients in this salad are already very flavorful, but possible additions include chopped pecans, a diced apple, or crumbled vegetarian goat cheese.

# Parsnip and Apple Soup

**SERVES 4 TO 6** / **PREP TIME:** 15 minutes / **COOK TIME:** 40 minutes

*As soon as the leaves begin to change colors, signifying the start of apple and root vegetable season, I make a batch of this flavorful soup. It's the kind of dish that warms you from the inside out, and every spoonful oozes coziness. Serve it with a large slice of crunchy bread and salted butter or on the side with grilled cheddar cheese sandwiches for an autumnal lunch.*

**2 tablespoons extra-virgin olive oil**

**2 shallots, diced**

**1 tablespoon fresh thyme leaves**

**5 parsnips, peeled and cut into ½-inch-thick rounds**

**3 apples, cored and diced**

**Salt**

**4 cups vegetable broth**

1. In a large stockpot or Dutch oven, warm the olive oil over medium-high heat.

2. Add the shallots, and cook for 3 to 5 minutes, or until softened.

3. Add the thyme, parsnips, and apples. Cook for 5 to 7 minutes, or until softened. Season with salt.

4. Add the broth, stir to combine, and bring to a boil.

5. Reduce the heat to medium-low. Cook for 20 to 25 minutes, or until the parsnips are fork-tender. Remove from the heat.

6. Using an immersion blender, puree the soup until smooth. Serve warm.

**NOTE:** My favorite types of apples to use in this recipe include Pink Lady and Honeycrisp or a combination of these with a Granny Smith apple. To blend the soup safely in a regular blender, fill it halfway, and puree the soup in batches. Leave a corner of the lid cracked, or remove the top of the blender and cover it with a folded dish towel to let steam escape as you blend. Be careful not to get burned by the hot steam.

# Mashed Parsnips with Mushroom and Lentil Gravy

**SERVES 4** / **PREP TIME:** 10 minutes / **COOK TIME:** 20 to 25 minutes

*You haven't given parsnips a full shot until you try them mashed. They have a similarly creamy texture to classic mashed potatoes, but offer a sweeter flavor. For a hearty cold weather meal, whip up a batch of these mashed parsnips, and smother them with a spoonful of the Mushroom and Lentil Gravy. Trust me, it's the perfect cure for the winter blues.*

**2 pounds parsnips, peeled and cut into 1-inch pieces**

**2 to 3 cups vegetable broth**

**½ cup whole milk**

**2 tablespoons unsalted butter**

**½ teaspoon salt, plus more as needed**

**Freshly ground black pepper**

**Mushroom and Lentil Gravy** (page 184)

1. Put the parsnips in a large pot. Pour in just enough broth to cover. Bring to a boil over high heat.

2. Reduce the heat to medium-low. Cover, and simmer for 12 to 15 minutes, or until the parsnips are tender.

3. Drain most of the broth, leaving about a third of it in the pot along with the parsnips. Place the pot back on the stove.

4. Stir in the milk, butter, and salt.

5. Increase the heat to medium. Cook for 2 to 3 minutes, or until the butter has melted and the milk is warm. Season with salt and pepper.

6. Using a potato masher, mash the parsnips in the pot. For a creamier texture, you can transfer the mixture to a blender, and blend until smooth. Remove from the heat.

7. Spoon the mash onto individual plates, and top with the gravy.

**NOTE:** Prep and cook times do not include the time needed to make the gravy. Make the gravy in advance and reheat, or prepare for longer prep and cook times if you are making the mash and gravy at the same time.

# Peas and Peapods

**Season:** spring

**Flavor profile:** Fresh green peas are deliciously sweet with earthy undertones and a starchy texture. Snow and sugar snap peas are typically eaten with their pods, which are crisp and fibrous.

**Pairs with:** butter, cream, ricotta cheese, parmesan cheese, garlic, shallots, carrots, asparagus, dill, mint, lemon, soy sauce, sesame oil, red pepper flakes

**Varieties:** green (garden), snow, sugar snap

**Preparation:** Trim pods before cooking or eating raw. To shell peas, use a knife or your fingers to pop open the pods and pluck out the peas.

**Favorite ways to serve:** raw, stir-fried, roasted

**Nutritional info:** Peas contain fiber, folate, iron, manganese, and vitamin C. They are also higher in protein than most other vegetables.

**Selection:** Choose peapods that are bright green and free from bruises or discoloration. Loose peas should be plump and firm without any evidence of shriveling.

**Storage:** Keep peapods in a sealed plastic bag or container in the refrigerator for up to five days. Shelled peas can be stored the same way if you plan to use them within a couple of days. Otherwise, blanch shelled peas for two minutes in boiling water, submerge them in ice water to cool, drain, and freeze in a plastic bag for up to three months.

# Roasted Sugar Snap Peas

**SERVES 4 / PREP TIME:** 5 minutes / **COOK TIME:** 10 minutes

1 pound sugar snap peas

1 tablespoon extra-virgin
  olive oil

Salt

Freshly ground
  black pepper

1. Preheat the oven to 450°F. Line a baking sheet with parchment paper or aluminum foil.

2. On the prepared baking sheet, toss the snap peas in the olive oil.

3. Spread the snap peas out in a single layer. Season with salt and pepper.

4. Transfer the baking sheet to the oven, and roast for 8 to 10 minutes, or until the snap peas are tender and browned. Remove from the oven.

NOTE: Other possible seasonings include a pinch of red pepper flakes and sesame seeds, garlic powder, or dried oregano and basil.

# Sautéed Green Peas with Dill and Parmesan

**SERVES 4** / **PREP TIME:** 5 minutes / **COOK TIME:** 10 minutes

*Peas are sometimes thought of as a mushy mess on a cafeteria tray, but when they're properly prepared, they add a crisp pop of flavor that's impossible to resist. With this recipe, you'll see what I mean in just 15 minutes. Freshly shaved parmesan cheese and a touch of fresh dill highlight the vegetal taste of fresh peas to make a perfect side dish.*

**1 tablespoon extra-virgin olive oil**

**3 garlic cloves, minced**

**2 cups green peas**

**1 tablespoon chopped fresh dill**

**Freshly ground black pepper**

**½ cup freshly shaved vegetarian parmesan cheese**

1. In a large skillet, warm the olive oil over medium heat.

2. Add the garlic and cook for about 2 minutes, or until fragrant.

3. Add the peas and dill. Season with pepper. Cook for 5 to 7 minutes, or until the peas are tender. Remove from the heat.

4. Serve the peas with the parmesan cheese.

**NOTE:** You can use fresh or frozen peas for this recipe. Frozen peas do not need to be thawed before adding to the skillet.

# Snap Pea and Edamame Stir-Fry

**SERVES 4** / **PREP TIME:** 10 minutes / **COOK TIME:** 10 minutes

*Sugar snap peas are my favorite ingredient in stir-fries, mainly because of their delightful crunch. This easy stir-fry combines them with equally crunchy carrots, protein-rich edamame, brown rice, and a simply delicious honey-soy sauce. For ultimate flavor, be sure to transfer every last drop of the sauce in the skillet onto your plate.*

### FOR THE STIR-FRY

1 tablespoon extra-virgin olive oil
1 tablespoon toasted sesame oil
2 cups sugar snap peas
1 cup thinly sliced carrots
1½ cups cooked edamame

### FOR THE SAUCE

3 tablespoons honey
3 tablespoons soy sauce
2 tablespoons rice vinegar
3 garlic cloves, minced
Salt

2 cups cooked brown rice

### TO MAKE THE STIR-FRY

1. In a large skillet or wok, warm the olive oil and sesame oil over medium-high heat.

2. Add the snap peas and carrots. Cook for 5 to 7 minutes, or until softened.

3. Stir in the edamame.

### TO MAKE THE SAUCE

4. While the vegetables are cooking, in a small bowl, whisk together the honey, soy sauce, vinegar, and garlic.

5. Pour the sauce over the vegetables and cook for 1 minute more, or until warmed through. Season with salt to taste. Remove from the heat.

6. Spoon the rice into bowls, and top with the stir-fry and sauce.

NOTE: You can add or substitute other types of vegetables in this dish, but keep it to 3 cups total to avoid overcrowding the pan. Use maple syrup in place of honey to make this dish vegan and tamari instead of soy sauce to make it gluten-free.

# Green Pea and Ricotta Spread

**MAKES ABOUT 2 CUPS** / **PREP TIME:** 5 minutes / **COOK TIME:** 10 minutes

*When garden peas start popping up at farmers' markets and grocery stores, I know that spring has officially sprung. After making it through a bitter Minnesota winter, the arrival of the first spring vegetables and the warm weather that accompanies them is especially exciting to me. I consider this creamy pea spread my transitional recipe to a new season of vegetables. It's the snack I make to enjoy with crackers and a glass of rosé on the first warm night of the year.*

**1 cup fresh or frozen peas**

**1 cup whole-milk vegetarian ricotta cheese**

**Juice of 1 lemon**

**1 heaping tablespoon chopped fresh mint**

**½ teaspoon salt, plus more as needed**

**Freshly ground black pepper**

1. Put the peas in a small saucepan with ¼ cup of water. Bring to a boil over high heat.

2. Reduce the heat to medium-low. Cover and cook for 5 to 7 minutes, or until the peas are tender. Remove from the heat. Drain in a colander and rinse for at least 30 seconds under cold running water.

3. In a high-powered blender or food processor, combine the peas, ricotta cheese, lemon juice, mint, and salt. Pulse until smooth. Season with salt and pepper to taste. (Alternatively, you can mash the ingredients together in a bowl with a fork if you want a chunkier spread.)

**NOTE:** Serve this spread with crackers or toasted baguette slices. You can also use it on vegetable wraps and open-face sandwiches like Watermelon Radish Toast (page 219). Store in an airtight container in the refrigerator for up to 4 days.

# Snap Pea and Barley Salad

**SERVES 4 TO 6 / PREP TIME:** 10 minutes

*This healthy grain-based salad may look overly simple, but it has a complex flavor profile thanks to the shallot dressing and combination of textures. Sugar snap peas provide a refreshing crispness that offsets the chewy consistency of barley and the buttery mouthfeel of chickpeas. With so much to offer, this recipe is bound to become your go-to weekday lunch.*

**2 cups cooked pearl barley**

**1 pound sugar snap peas, trimmed and halved**

**1 (15-ounce) can chickpeas, drained and rinsed**

**Shallot-Dijon Vinaigrette** (page 233)

1. In a large bowl, mix together the barley, snap peas, and chickpeas.

2. Add the vinaigrette and toss until evenly coated. Serve immediately, or refrigerate for a while to make it colder.

**NOTE:** Cook barley according to the package instructions. Trader Joe's and other stores offer quick-cooking varieties that can save you time. You can prep both the barley and dressing in advance and put the salad together when you're ready to eat. Leftovers can be stored in an airtight container in the refrigerator for up to 5 days.

# Peppers

**Season:** summer

**Flavor profile:** Ranging from sweet and mild to spicy and hot, the flavor profile of peppers largely depends on the type. Pepper seeds, especially from jalapeño or serrano peppers, contribute additional heat if they're not removed. In terms of texture, peppers have crunchy, juicy flesh.

**Pairs with:** fresh herbs, lime, red wine vinegar, cheese, hummus, garlic, black beans, pinto beans

**Varieties:** green, red, yellow, and orange bell peppers; jalapeño; serrano; habanero

**Preparation:** Cut off the stem, then cut in half. Remove the seeds with a spoon, knife, or your hands (be careful not to touch your face after cutting spicy peppers). Bell peppers can be diced or cut into strips, whereas spicy peppers should be more finely chopped.

**Favorite ways to serve:** raw, roasted, sautéed

**Nutritional info:** All types of peppers contain several vitamins and minerals, including high amounts of vitamin C. The compound in hot peppers that makes them spicy, known as capsaicin, may help improve digestion and relieve pain.

**Selection:** Fresh peppers have firm, glossy skin and feel heavy for their size. They should have no brown or black spots.

**Storage:** Keep peppers dry to prevent rotting. Put them in a sealed plastic bag, or wrap tightly with plastic wrap, and store in the vegetable drawer of the refrigerator for up to five days.

# Roasted Red Peppers

**SERVES 4 TO 6 / PREP TIME:** 10 minutes / **COOK TIME:** 25 minutes

**4 red bell peppers, halved and seeded**

**¼ cup extra-virgin olive oil**

**3 garlic cloves, minced**

**Salt**

**Freshly ground black pepper**

1. Preheat the oven to 450°F. Line a baking sheet with aluminum foil.

2. Arrange the bell peppers, cut-side down, in a single layer on the prepared baking sheet.

3. Transfer the baking sheet to the oven, and roast for 20 to 25 minutes, or until the peppers are wilted and charred. Remove from the oven. Let cool for a few minutes.

4. Rinse each pepper under cold water, and using your fingers, peel off the skin. Transfer to a cutting board, and cut into thin slices. Put into a glass jar with a lid or into an airtight container.

5. Add the olive oil and garlic. Season with salt and pepper.

6. Seal the lid, and shake to combine.

**NOTE:** The peppers will keep in the refrigerator for up to 2 weeks. You can also freeze them in zip-top plastic bags for up to 3 months.

# Fresh Bell Pepper and Herb Salad

**SERVES 4 / PREP TIME:** 15 to 20 minutes

*If you have a vegetable garden with pepper plants and herbs during the warm months, this recipe is a wonderful way to enjoy the fruits of your labor. Crunchy, refreshing bell peppers combined with a variety of herbs make for an irresistibly fresh salad that captures the essence of the summer harvest. I love to use a mix of red, orange, or yellow bell peppers to make the dish as colorful as possible.*

### FOR THE SALAD

**2 large bell peppers, seeded and cut into rings**
**1 small shallot, cut into rings**
**¼ cup red wine vinegar**
**Salt**

### FOR THE DRESSING

**1 tablespoon extra-virgin olive oil**
**1 tablespoon chopped fresh mint**
**1 tablespoon chopped fresh basil**
**1 tablespoon chopped fresh parsley**
**1 tablespoon chopped fresh dill**

### TO MAKE THE SALAD

1. In a large bowl, toss the bell peppers and shallots in the vinegar. Season with salt.

2. Let the salad sit for about 10 minutes so that the vinegar softens the peppers, if desired.

### TO MAKE THE DRESSING

3. In a small bowl, mix together the olive oil, mint, basil, parsley, and dill.

4. Add the dressing to the salad and toss until evenly coated.

**NOTE:** This salad tastes even better after it sits in the refrigerator for a couple of hours to let the flavors meld together. You can store it in an airtight container in the refrigerator for up to 1 day in advance for maximum flavor.

# Stuffed Pepper Soup

**SERVES 4 TO 6** / **PREP TIME:** 10 minutes / **COOK TIME:** 40 minutes

*For the same delicious flavors of stuffed peppers without the hassle of eating them with a fork and knife, I give you stuffed pepper soup. This low-maintenance dish calls for mostly pantry staples plus fresh bell peppers. With plenty of vegetables, brown rice, and pinto beans, it's a nutritious and balanced meal in one bowl. I like to top mine with shredded vegetarian Mexican cheese, a dollop of sour cream, and diced avocado.*

**1 tablespoon extra-virgin olive oil**

**1 yellow onion, diced**

**4 garlic cloves, minced**

**½ teaspoon salt, plus more as needed**

**2 bell peppers, seeded and diced**

**1 (14-ounce) can fire-roasted diced tomatoes**

**½ teaspoon dried oregano**

**½ teaspoon dried thyme**

**1 cup short-grain brown rice**

**4 cups vegetable broth**

**1 (15-ounce) can pinto beans, drained and rinsed**

1. In a large pot, warm the olive oil over medium heat.

2. Add the onion, garlic, and salt. Cook for 3 to 4 minutes, or until fragrant.

3. Add the bell peppers, tomatoes, oregano, and thyme. Cook for 3 to 4 minutes, or until softened.

4. Stir in the rice and broth. Bring to a boil.

5. Reduce the heat to medium-low. Simmer, stirring occasionally, for about 30 minutes, or until the rice is tender.

6. Stir in the beans. Season with salt to taste. Remove from the heat. Ladle into bowls, and serve.

**NOTE:** If you don't eat all of the soup right away, the rice will continue to absorb the liquid. Add some more broth or water when reheating. Leftovers can be stored in an airtight container in the refrigerator for up to 4 days.

# Pickled Jalapeños

**MAKES 2 (16-OUNCE) JARS** / **PREP TIME:** 10 minutes / **COOK TIME:** 5 minutes

*I always thought jalapeños were too spicy until I tried them pickled. If you shy away from their heat like me, give this recipe a try. When soaked in a basic vinegar brine, jalapeños become sweeter and milder. Enjoy them on sandwiches, nachos, tacos, and eggs. Pickling jalapeños is also a great way to preserve a large harvest, CSA share, or farmers' market haul.*

**10 jalapeño peppers, thinly sliced**
**4 garlic cloves, smashed**
**1 cup white vinegar**
**¼ cup sugar**
**1 tablespoon salt**

1. Divide the jalapeños and garlic equally between 2 (16-ounce) jars with lids.

2. In a small saucepan, combine the vinegar, sugar, salt, and 1 cup of water. Bring to a simmer over low heat, and stir until the sugar dissolves. Remove from the heat.

3. Carefully divide the brine between the jars.

4. Seal the lids. Let the jalapeños cool to room temperature and transfer to the refrigerator.

**NOTE:** Pickled jalapeños will last for about two weeks in the refrigerator. If your fingers get irritated from handling jalapeños, wear gloves when slicing them.

# Potatoes

**Season:** fall, winter

**Flavor profile:** Plain potatoes have an earthy taste that's especially concentrated in the skin and starchy flesh that becomes tender when cooked. Potatoes are most commonly enjoyed mashed, fried, or stuffed with butter, cheese, salt, and other fixins that have made them an iconic comfort food.

**Pairs with:** cheese, sour cream, butter, salt, leeks, shallots, onion, garlic, broccoli, rosemary, chives, chili powder, paprika

**Varieties:** Russet, red, Yukon Gold, fingerling, purple, new, and several other varieties

**Preparation:** Scrub clean with a vegetable brush. Keep potatoes whole, slice with a mandoline for chips, or dice.

Remove the skin with a swivel peeler if desired.

**Favorite ways to serve:** baked, made into chips and fries, mashed

**Nutritional info:** Due to their starch content, potatoes are high in carbo-hydrates and very filling. They are also an excellent source of potassium, a mineral that's necessary for blood pressure regulation.

**Selection:** Look for potatoes that are firm to the touch with no dark spots. Sprouts on the skin of potatoes are harmless but do indicate that they're older and should be removed before cooking. Avoid potatoes that have a green tinge since they contain the toxic compound solanine.

**Storage:** Keep potatoes in a mesh or paper bag, basket, or cardboard box in a cool, dry, and dark place. They can last for at least a couple of weeks and sometimes longer.

# Shortcut Baked Potatoes

**SERVES 4 / PREP TIME:** 5 minutes / **COOK TIME:** 35 minutes

1 tablespoon extra-virgin
olive oil

4 Russet potatoes,
halved lengthwise

Salt

Salted butter, sour cream,
or chopped chives,
for serving

1. Preheat the oven to 400°F. Line a baking sheet with parchment paper.

2. Brush the parchment paper and both sides of the potatoes with the olive oil.

3. Arrange the potatoes, cut-side down, on the prepared baking sheet. Season with salt.

4. Transfer the baking sheet to the oven and bake for 30 to 35 minutes, or until the potatoes are tender and crispy. Remove from the oven.

5. Serve the potatoes with butter, sour cream, or chives.

**NOTE:** You can also stuff them with chili or top them with gravy.

# Favorite Mashed Potatoes with Pan-Fried Shallots

**SERVES 6** / **PREP TIME:** 10 minutes / **COOK TIME:** 25 minutes

*Is there a better comfort food than mashed potatoes? Every time I cook this beloved dish, the distinct aroma and creamy texture bring back a flood of happy memories involving family meals and holiday gatherings. Besides the spuds, the most important ingredient in my rendition of mashed potatoes is sour cream. It contributes a slightly tangy taste and the perfect amount of rich flavor.*

**3 pounds potatoes, cut into 2-inch pieces**

**1½ cups milk**

**3 tablespoons unsalted butter**

**½ cup sour cream**

**Salt**

**Freshly ground black pepper**

**Pan-Fried Shallots**
(page 232)

1. Put the potatoes in a large pot, and cover with water. Bring to a boil over high heat.

2. Reduce the heat to a simmer. Cook for 12 to 15 minutes, or until the potatoes are fork-tender. Drain, and return to the pot or transfer to a large bowl.

3. In a small saucepan, warm the milk and butter over low heat until the butter has melted. Remove from the heat.

4. Pour the mixture over the potatoes.

5. Add the sour cream. Season with salt and pepper.

6. Using a hand mixer or potato masher, mash the potatoes to your desired texture. Season with salt and pepper to taste.

7. Serve the mashed potatoes warm, topped with pan-fried shallots.

**NOTE:** Yukon Gold and Russet are my favorite types to use for mashed potatoes. You can peel the potatoes if desired, but I prefer to leave the skins on.

# Potato and Leek French Bread Tartine

**SERVES 4 TO 6** / **PREP TIME:** 10 minutes / **COOK TIME:** 30 to 35 minutes

*Potatoes and leeks are a culinary match made in heaven, especially for warm meals that help take the chilly edge off cold winter nights. These crispy squares highlight the complementary flavors of a classic vegetable duo. Toasted French bread serves as a base for tender leeks and crispy potatoes snuggled between blankets of melted gruyère. Make this recipe for a snack, appetizer, or dinner.*

**4 tablespoons extra-virgin olive oil, divided, plus more as needed**

**3 garlic cloves, minced**

**1 loaf French bread, halved lengthwise**

**1 Yukon Gold potato, quartered lengthwise and cut into ¼-inch-thick slices**

**1 leek, white and light green parts, thinly sliced**

**Salt**

**Freshly ground black pepper**

**2 cups freshly grated vegetarian gruyère cheese, divided**

**2 tablespoons chopped fresh rosemary**

1. Preheat the oven to 400°F. Line a baking sheet with parchment paper.

2. In a small bowl, whisk together 2 tablespoons of olive oil and the garlic.

3. Brush the bread with the oil mixture and transfer to the prepared baking sheet.

4. In a large skillet, warm the remaining 2 tablespoons of olive oil over medium heat.

5. Arrange the potato in a single layer in the skillet. Cook for 10 to 12 minutes, flipping as best you can halfway through, or until browned and tender.

6. Add the leek and a drizzle of olive oil as needed. Cook for 3 to 4 minutes, or until the leek has softened and the potato is crispy. Season with salt and pepper. Remove from the heat.

7. Transfer the baking sheet to the oven and bake for 3 to 4 minutes, or until the bread is lightly toasted. Remove from the oven.

CONTINUED

8. Sprinkle about 1 cup of gruyère cheese on top of the bread.

9. Arrange the potato and leek on top of the cheese.

10. Sprinkle the remaining 1 cup of cheese and the rosemary on top.

11. Transfer the baking sheet to the oven, and bake for 10 to 12 minutes, or until the cheese has melted and the edges are crispy. Remove from the oven. Transfer to a cutting board, and cut into squares.

NOTE: Long, wide loaves of French bread have the most surface area for spreading the toppings. Feel free to use other types of artisan bread loaves with similar shapes.

# Parmesan-Roasted Fingerlings with Fried Eggs

**SERVES 4** / **PREP TIME:** 5 minutes / **COOK TIME:** 40 minutes

*The slender, stubby shape of fingerling potatoes makes them the perfect size to coat with a layer of parmesan cheese and crisp up in the oven. Though these aren't your classic French fries, they have a similarly crispy skin and salty flavor. You can enjoy roasted fingerlings on their own as a side dish or top them with fried eggs for a breakfast hash of sorts.*

2 pounds fingerling
   potatoes, large ones
   halved lengthwise

3 tablespoons extra-virgin
   olive oil, plus more
   as needed

Salt

Freshly ground
   black pepper

⅓ cup freshly
   grated vegetarian
   parmesan cheese

4 to 8 large eggs, cooked
   to your liking

1. Preheat the oven to 400°F. Line a baking sheet with parchment paper.

2. In a large mixing bowl, toss the potatoes with the olive oil. Season with salt and pepper.

3. Spread the potatoes out in a single layer on the baking sheet. Reserve the bowl for later use.

4. Transfer the baking sheet to the oven, and bake for 15 to 20 minutes, or until the potatoes are tender but not yet browned. Remove from the oven.

5. Return the potatoes to the bowl. Toss with the parmesan cheese until evenly coated. Add a drizzle of olive oil as needed.

6. Spread the potatoes out on the baking sheet again.

7. Return the baking sheet to the oven, and bake for 15 to 20 minutes, or until the potatoes are crispy. Remove from the oven.

8. Serve the potatoes with the eggs on top.

**NOTE:** For more flavor, add a teaspoon of garlic powder to the parmesan cheese before tossing with the potatoes. You can also add chopped fresh dill or rosemary, smoked paprika, or red pepper flakes to mix it up.

# Paprika-Baked Potato Chips

**SERVES 4** / **PREP TIME:** 10 minutes / **COOK TIME:** 20 minutes

*Potato chips rank high on my list of favorite snacks, and I've been determined to figure out the best recipe for homemade chips over the past few years. Based on my experimentation, it's key to thinly slice the potatoes, use a high-starch variety like Russet, and coat the chips with just enough oil before they go into the oven. Following those tips will yield a crunchy snack that most closely mimics store-bought chips.*

**3 teaspoons extra-virgin olive oil, divided**

**1 Russet potato, thinly sliced with a mandoline**

**1 teaspoon smoked paprika**

**Salt**

1. Preheat the oven to 400°F. Line 2 baking sheets with parchment paper. Brush the parchment paper with about 1 teaspoon of olive oil.

2. On the prepared baking sheets, brush the potato with the remaining 2 teaspoons of olive oil, coating each slice with a very thin layer of oil.

3. Arrange the potato in a single layer.

4. Transfer the baking sheets to the oven and bake for 20 minutes, flipping the potato over and rotating the sheets halfway through, or until the edges are crispy. Some of the chips may cook faster than others, so keep an eye and take them off the sheets early as needed. Remove from the oven. Let cool for 5 minutes. Transfer to a bowl.

5. Add the paprika, season with salt to taste, and toss.

**NOTE:** Using a mandoline is the best way to cut the potatoes into very thin slices for this recipe, but you can also use a sharp knife. These chips are best enjoyed right away, since they will lose crispiness over time.

# Purple Potato Salad

**SERVES 4 TO 6** / **PREP TIME:** 10 minutes / **COOK TIME:** 20 minutes

*The beautiful flesh of purple potatoes makes this recipe a real stunner, but it's more than just a pretty face. Purple potatoes get their color from anthocyanins, pigments that act as antioxidants in the body and may help improve vision and boost heart health. Plus, this dish swaps in olive oil for the traditional mayonnaise for a lighter twist on classic potato salad. It's one of my go-to recipes for potlucks, cookouts, and holidays.*

**2 pounds purple potatoes, cut into bite-size pieces**

**Salt**

**¼ cup extra-virgin olive oil**

**1 tablespoon Dijon mustard**

**1 tablespoon white wine vinegar**

**2 tablespoons chopped fresh dill**

**Freshly ground black pepper**

1. Put the potatoes in a large pot, cover with water, and add a few pinches salt. Bring to a boil.

2. Reduce the heat to medium-low. Cook for 6 to 8 minutes, or until the potatoes are fork-tender. Remove from the heat. Drain.

3. In a large bowl, whisk together the olive oil, mustard, vinegar, and dill.

4. Add the potatoes and toss until evenly coated. Season with salt and pepper to taste.

**NOTE:** You can substitute the juice of ½ lemon for the white wine vinegar.

# Radishes

**Season:** spring, winter

**Flavor profile:** Raw radishes are peppery and slightly spicy, contributing a wonderful crunch and a zesty punch to dishes. Cooked radishes are tender and mellow. Radish leaves are also edible and can be used in pesto, stir-fries, and other dishes.

**Pairs with:** dill, rosemary, mint, lemon, vinegars, sea salt, bread, butter, whole grains

**Varieties:** red, pink, purple, white, black, daikon, watermelon

**Preparation:** Trim off the leaves, and scrub the roots clean. Use whole, thinly slice with a mandoline, or chop into pieces.

**Favorite ways to serve:** shaved or grated, roasted, pickled

**Nutritional info:** Radishes are rich in fiber and provide small amounts of potassium and vitamin C. They also contain compounds that have been shown to prevent cancer cell growth in test tube studies.

**Selection:** Choose radishes that feel firm, have smooth skin, and are bright in color. If their leaves are attached, they should be free of yellow spots and should not be wilting.

**Storage:** Use your hands to pluck the radishes from their greens. Wrap the loose radishes in a damp paper towel, and keep in a sealed plastic bag for up to two weeks. Store radishes that have already been cut in an airtight container covered with water to keep them crisp.

# Watermelon Radish Toast

**SERVES 4** / **PREP TIME:** 5 minutes

*Radish toast is a delightfully crunchy breakfast or lunch. In this rendition, toasted sourdough is topped with a generous schmear of Green Pea and Ricotta Spread that contributes fresh, creamy, and sweet undertones to help mellow the spicy radishes. I recommend using watermelon radishes to add a beautiful pop of color, but any variety of radish will do.*

**½ cup Green Pea and Ricotta Spread** (page 203)

**4 thick sourdough bread slices, toasted**

**1 small watermelon radish, thinly sliced**

**¼ cup chopped almonds**

**Squeeze of lemon juice** (optional)

1. Spread 2 tablespoons of ricotta spread on each slice of bread.

2. Arrange the radish slices on top, sprinkle with the almonds, and drizzle with fresh lemon juice (if using).

**NOTE:** Cut the radishes and make the ricotta spread in advance so you can put this dish together quickly. This recipe also tastes good with a drizzle of plain or Garlic-Infused Honey (page 134).

# Tarragon-Roasted Radishes

**SERVES 4** / **PREP TIME:** 10 minutes / **COOK TIME:** 30 minutes

**2 bunches radishes, trimmed**

**1 tablespoon extra-virgin olive oil**

**2 tablespoons chopped fresh tarragon**

**Salt**

**Freshly ground black pepper**

1. Preheat the oven to 400°F. Line a baking sheet with parchment paper.

2. On the prepared baking sheet, toss the radishes with the olive oil and tarragon.

3. Spread the radishes out in a single layer. Season with salt and pepper.

4. Transfer the baking sheet to the oven and bake for 25 to 30 minutes, or until the radishes are fork-tender. Remove from the oven.

# Cold Radish Soup

**SERVES 4 TO 6 / PREP TIME:** 20 minutes / **COOK TIME:** 10 minutes

*I first tried this cold soup when my mother-in-law Jenny served it to me, using a recipe that her friend Gail made for their book club. It's based on a similar type of soup that's commonly consumed in Russia. With a tangy kefir base, crunchy radishes and cucumber, starchy potatoes, and fresh dill, it's incredibly refreshing and flavorful. Plus, you don't have to blow on every spoonful to cool it down!*

**3 small red potatoes, diced**

**1 bunch radishes, trimmed and diced**

**2 scallions, green and white parts, thinly sliced**

**1 cucumber, peeled, seeded, and diced**

**4 cups plain whole-milk kefir**

**Juice of ½ lemon**

**¼ cup chopped fresh dill**

**4 hard-boiled eggs, peeled and diced**

**Salt**

**Freshly ground black pepper**

1. Fill a large pot with 2 to 3 inches of water. Place a steamer basket inside the pot, and put the potatoes inside the basket. Bring the water to a boil over high heat. Cover, reduce the heat to medium, and cook for 7 to 10 minutes, or until tender. Remove from the heat. Transfer to a large bowl.

2. Add the radishes, scallions, and cucumber. Toss to combine.

3. In a separate bowl, whisk together the kefir, lemon juice, dill, and additional water to thin the kefir as needed.

4. Pour the kefir mixture over the potatoes and other vegetables, and mix together.

5. Stir in the eggs. Season with salt and pepper to taste. Spoon the soup into bowls for serving.

**NOTE:** If you don't have a steamer basket, you can boil the potatoes whole and then dice them. Serve this soup on its own or with crunchy croutons or bread. If you are making it in advance, wait to add the diced eggs until right before serving. If the eggs sit in the soup for too long, they may contribute a subtle sulfur taste.

# Radish Chips

**SERVES 4** / **PREP TIME:** 5 minutes / **COOK TIME:** 15 minutes

*These simple veggie chips make a great snack for after school or work. They taste delicious with just a sprinkle of salt and pepper, and you can have them on the table in only 20 minutes. If there are any left after you satisfy your snack attack (doubtful), throw them on salads, add them to a cheese board, or dip in hummus.*

**3 bunches radishes, thinly sliced**

**1 tablespoon extra-virgin olive oil**

**Salt**

**Freshly ground black pepper**

1. Preheat the oven to 400°F. Line 2 baking sheets with parchment paper.

2. In a large bowl, toss the radishes with the olive oil until very lightly coated.

3. Spread the radishes out in a single layer on the prepared baking sheets.

4. Transfer the baking sheets to the oven, and bake for 12 to 15 minutes, or until the radishes are crispy and wrinkled. Check on them frequently, starting at 10 minutes, to make sure they don't burn. Remove from the oven. Let cool for a couple of minutes. Season with salt and pepper.

**NOTE:** A mandoline works best for slicing the radishes thinly, but you can also use a sharp knife. For a spicy kick, sprinkle with a pinch of cayenne pepper before eating.

# Rhubarb

**Season:** spring

**Flavor profile:** Although it may look like a pink version of celery, rhubarb has a distinct taste. Raw rhubarb is tart and sour, whereas cooked rhubarb is sweeter and therefore commonly used in desserts. Recipes with rhubarb only call for the stalks, since the leaves are toxic and contain oxalic acid, which can damage the kidneys when consumed in high amounts.

**Pairs with:** strawberries, blueberries, sugar and other sweeteners, oats, ice cream, lemon, red onion, orange

**Varieties:** can be predominantly red, pink, or green, or a combination of these colors

**Preparation:** Use a knife to cut off the leaves and ends of the stalks. Rinse under cold water to clean, and cut into ½-inch-thick to 1-inch-thick slices, similar to how you would prepare celery.

**Favorite ways to serve:** baked into desserts, cooked down into jams and chutneys

**Nutritional info:** Rhubarb provides fiber, bone-building calcium, and vitamin K, which assists in blood clotting. Although plain rhubarb is very nutritious, most desserts that feature it are high in added sugar.

**Selection:** Rhubarb stalks should be firm, with healthy ends that do not look dried out. Floppy stalks are a sign that the rhubarb is old.

**Storage:** Store rhubarb stalks in a sealed bag or wrapped in plastic wrap in the refrigerator for up to one week. You can extend the short rhubarb season by buying in bulk and freezing for later. Cut the stalks into pieces, lay them on a plate, transfer to the freezer for a few hours until firm, then keep them in zip-top plastic freezer bags for several months.

# Rhubarb and Candied Ginger Jam

**MAKES ABOUT 3 CUPS / PREP TIME:** 5 minutes, plus 20 minutes to macerate /
**COOK TIME:** 20 minutes

**4 cups ½-inch-thick
  rhubarb slices**
**1½ cups granulated sugar**
**Zest and juice of 1 lemon**
**¼ cup finely chopped
  Homemade Candied
  Ginger** (page 140)

1. In a large bowl, mix together the rhubarb, sugar, lemon zest and juice, and candied ginger. Let sit for about 20 minutes, or until the rhubarb releases its juices.

2. Transfer the mixture to a saucepan. Bring to a boil, stirring frequently, over medium-high heat.

3. Reduce the heat to medium. Simmer for 15 to 20 minutes, or until the jam thickens. Remove from the heat. Transfer to glass jars. Let cool to room temperature.

4. Seal the lids tightly, and transfer the jars to the refrigerator.

**NOTE:** Store the jam in the refrigerator for up to 3 weeks. Serve on toast, biscuits, crackers, or swirled into yogurt.

# Fresh Berry and Rhubarb Crisp

**SERVES 6** / **PREP TIME:** 10 minutes / **COOK TIME:** 30 minutes

*Berry crisp is an all-star dessert on its own, but adding tangy rhubarb brings it to a whole new level. This classic springtime treat combines the gooey deliciousness of warm berries with a crunchy oat topping. Serve it with a dollop of whipped cream or a scoop of ice cream, and you'll be instantly wishing rhubarb season was longer.*

**FOR THE FILLING**

Nonstick cooking spray
2 cups diced rhubarb
1 cup sliced
  fresh strawberries
1 cup fresh blueberries
½ cup granulated sugar
1 tablespoon cornstarch

**FOR THE TOPPING**

1 cup all-purpose flour
1 cup old-fashioned oats
¾ cup packed light
  brown sugar
8 tablespoons (1 stick)
  unsalted butter, melted
1 teaspoon ground
  cinnamon
½ teaspoon salt

**TO MAKE THE FILLING**

1. Preheat the oven to 350°F. Grease a 9-by-13-inch baking dish.

2. In the prepared baking dish, combine the rhubarb, strawberries, blueberries, sugar, and cornstarch. Pour in ¼ cup of water, and stir to combine.

**TO MAKE THE TOPPING**

3. In a medium bowl, mix together the flour, oats, sugar, butter, cinnamon, and salt.

4. Spoon the mixture on top of the filling.

5. Transfer the baking dish to the oven and bake for 25 to 30 minutes, or until the topping has browned and the berries are bubbling. Remove from the oven. Let cool for a few minutes before serving.

NOTE: You can use frozen rhubarb or berries in place of fresh. If needed, gluten-free all-purpose flour also works in this recipe.

# Rutabaga

**Season:** fall, winter

**Flavor profile:** Rutabagas, also known as swede, taste like a cross between turnips and Yukon Gold potatoes. Cooking transforms their slightly bitter flavor and brings out sweet and savory undertones. The texture of rutabaga is crispy like a carrot when raw and creamy when cooked.

**Pairs with:** milk, cream, butter, apples, pears, onions, potatoes, carrots, garlic, mustard, walnuts, brown sugar, rosemary, thyme

**Varieties:** several that all have a purple top and a golden yellow root

**Preparation:** Trim the ends, scrub clean with a vegetable brush, peel if desired, and cut into pieces.

**Favorite ways to serve:** grated, shaved, roasted, mashed

**Nutritional info:** Rutabaga are especially rich in anti-aging vitamin C, as well as potassium, magnesium, and calcium, which work together to maintain healthy blood pressure.

**Selection:** Look for rutabagas that are firm and unblemished. Although small cuts around the top are normal, they should not have large slashes on their skin.

**Storage:** Put rutabagas unwashed in a sealed plastic bag or container in the refrigerator. They typically last for two weeks or sometimes longer.

# Shaved Rutabaga and Peanut Salad

**SERVES 4 / PREP TIME:** 10 minutes

## FOR THE DRESSING

3 tablespoons extra-virgin
   olive oil
1 tablespoon rice vinegar
Juice of 1 lime
2 teaspoons honey

## FOR THE SALAD

1 rutabaga, peeled and
   shaved into thin slices
   with a mandoline
2 scallions, green and
   white parts, thinly sliced
¼ cup chopped peanuts
2 tablespoons chopped
   fresh cilantro

## TO MAKE THE DRESSING

1. In a large bowl, whisk together the olive oil, vinegar, lime juice, and honey until smooth.

## TO MAKE THE SALAD

2. Add the rutabaga, scallions, peanuts, and cilantro. Toss until evenly coated.

# Rutabaga and Parsnip Gratin

**SERVES 6** / **PREP TIME:** 15 minutes / **COOK TIME:** 45 to 55 minutes

*Made with a base of rutabaga and parsnips coated in a rich, savory sauce, this root vegetable gratin showcases just how decadent vegetables can be. Instead of making classic potato gratin for Thanksgiving or Christmas, try this seasonal twist instead. It's a great way to introduce some less common vegetables to the table and celebrate all that the winter harvest has to offer.*

**1 rutabaga, peeled and thinly sliced**

**3 parsnips, peeled and thinly sliced**

**6 tablespoons extra-virgin olive oil, divided**

**1 shallot, diced**

**2 tablespoons salted butter**

**2 tablespoons fresh thyme leaves**

**¾ cup vegetable broth**

**½ cup freshly grated vegetarian gruyère cheese**

1. Preheat the oven to 400°F. Grease a 12-inch cast-iron or other oven-safe skillet.

2. Arrange the rutabaga and parsnips in alternating layers in the skillet.

3. In another skillet, warm 2 tablespoons of olive oil over medium heat.

4. Add the shallot, and cook for 3 to 4 minutes, or until softened. Remove from the heat.

5. Add the remaining 4 tablespoons of olive oil, the butter, thyme, and broth. Whisk until the butter has melted.

6. Carefully pour the sauce over the layered vegetables.

7. Cover the skillet with an oven-safe lid or aluminum foil. Transfer to the oven, and bake for 30 to 35 minutes.

8. Remove the lid, and sprinkle the gruyère cheese on top. Bake, uncovered, for 10 to 15 minutes, or until the cheese has melted and the vegetables are very tender. Remove from the oven. Serve warm.

**NOTE:** You can use this recipe as a base and substitute other root vegetables, such as beets, turnips, and carrots.

# Rutabaga Breakfast Hash

**SERVES 4** / **PREP TIME:** 5 minutes / **COOK TIME:** 25 minutes

*With a similar texture and color, rutabagas are a good substitute for breakfast potatoes. In fact, since rutabagas are lower in starch, they're easier to cook in a skillet and don't stick to the pan as much. This one-pan hash features diced rutabaga seasoned with smoked paprika and topped with eggs. Though it's delicious on its own, adding mushroom chorizo (see page 181) brings the recipe up a notch.*

**2 tablespoons extra-virgin olive oil**

**½ yellow onion, diced**

**1 rutabaga, peeled and finely diced**

**2 teaspoons smoked paprika**

**½ teaspoon salt**

**½ teaspoon freshly ground black pepper**

**4 large eggs**

1. In a large cast-iron skillet or other oven-safe pan, warm the olive oil over medium heat.

2. Add the onion, and cook for 3 to 4 minutes, or until softened.

3. Add the rutabaga, paprika, salt, and pepper. Cook, stirring every few minutes, for 12 to 15 minutes, or until browned and tender. Remove from the heat.

4. Turn the broiler to high.

5. Using a spoon, make 4 wells in the hash.

6. Crack an egg into each well and transfer the skillet to the oven. Cook for 2 to 3 minutes, or until the eggs reach your desired doneness. Remove from the oven. Enjoy warm.

**NOTE:** Other possible additions include diced bell peppers, cotija cheese (note that cotija is made with animal rennet), Pickled Jalapeños (page 209), or Arugula Salsa Verde (page 18).

# Shallots

**Season:** fall

**Flavor profile:** Shallots are a type of onion, but they grow in bulbs similar to garlic with multiple large cloves. Their taste is also sweeter and subtler than onions. In fact, sautéed shallots that have been cooked down or caramelized have a pronounced sweet-savory flavor.

**Pairs with:** olive oil, butter, garlic, thyme, rosemary, balsamic vinegar, mustard

**Varieties:** pink, red, gray, yellow

**Preparation:** Trim off the tops, and pull apart the large cloves. Remove the papery skin, and dice or cut into thin slices. Discard the ends.

**Favorite ways to serve:** fried, sautéed, raw

**Nutritional info:** As a relative of onions and garlic, shallots have a similar nutritional profile. They contain a number of beneficial sulfur-containing compounds that may exhibit anti-cancer effects.

**Selection:** When selecting shallots, follow the same tips as you would for choosing fresh onions or garlic. Shallots should feel firm and heavy, without any soft spots or sprouting.

**Storage:** Store shallots in a cool, dry place in the kitchen for up to three weeks or sometimes longer.

# Pan-Fried Shallots

**SERVES 4** / **PREP TIME:** 5 minutes / **COOK TIME:** 15 minutes

¼ **cup canola oil**

**2 shallots, thinly sliced**

1. In a skillet, warm the oil over medium heat. Line a plate with paper towels.

2. Add the shallots, and cook, stirring occasionally, for 10 to 15 minutes, or until browned and crispy. Reduce the heat as needed if the shallots cook too quickly. Remove from the heat. Transfer to the prepared plate, and let cool.

**NOTE:** Enjoy on sandwiches, veggie burgers, mashed potatoes, and more.

# Shallot-Dijon Vinaigrette

**MAKES ABOUT ½ CUP / PREP TIME:** 5 minutes

*Out of all the salad dressings I've made, I always come back to this tried-and-true shallot vinaigrette. It's equal parts zesty and tangy and goes with just about anything. Drizzle this all-purpose condiment on mixed greens and grain salads, or use it as a marinade for grilled vegetables. I'm sure you will find many delicious ways to take advantage of this recipe's versatility.*

**1 small shallot, finely chopped**

**¼ cup extra-virgin olive oil**

**1 tablespoon Dijon mustard**

**Juice of 1 lemon**

**¼ teaspoon salt**

1. In a small jar, mix together the shallot, olive oil, mustard, lemon juice, and salt.

2. Seal the lid, and shake until combined.

NOTE: The dressing can be refrigerated for up to 1 week and sometimes a little longer. Shake before using. For an extra kick, add 1 or 2 minced garlic cloves.

# French Lentil and Shallot Soup

**SERVES 4 TO 6** / **PREP TIME:** 15 minutes / **COOK TIME:** 45 minutes

*This mouthwatering dish is reminiscent of traditional French onion soup but with fully vegetarian ingredients and a shorter cook time. Sliced shallots are quickly caramelized before they simmer with lentils in a rich vegetable broth spiked with Worcestershire sauce. Be sure to serve this soup with a toasted French baguette to soak up every last drop.*

**2 tablespoons
salted butter**

**2 tablespoons extra-virgin
olive oil**

**6 shallots, thinly sliced**

**2 garlic cloves, minced**

**1 teaspoon dried thyme**

**2 tablespoons
all-purpose flour**

**6 cups vegetable broth**

**1 tablespoon vegan
Worcestershire sauce**

**2 bay leaves**

**1 cup French lentils,
sorted and rinsed**

1. In a large stockpot, warm the butter and olive oil over medium heat.

2. Add the shallots, and cook for 10 to 15 minutes, or until tender and slightly caramelized.

3. Add the garlic, thyme, and flour. Cook, stirring to coat the shallots in the flour, for 3 to 4 minutes, or until the garlic is fragrant.

4. Increase the heat to medium-high. Add the broth, Worcestershire sauce, bay leaves, and lentils. Bring to a boil.

5. Reduce the heat to medium-low. Cover and simmer for 20 to 25 minutes, or until the lentils are tender. Remove from the heat. Remove and discard the bay leaves before serving.

**NOTE:** For additional flavor, add ½ cup white wine and 1 tablespoon balsamic vinegar when you add the broth. You can also serve the soup with grated vegetarian gruyère cheese. Omit the butter and use double the olive oil if you want or need this to be vegan.

# Shallot Marmalade

**MAKES ABOUT 2 TO 3 CUPS** / **PREP TIME:** 15 minutes / **COOK TIME:** 20 minutes

*If you love the taste of shallots, you will be blown away by this four-ingredient, sweet and tangy marmalade. It has such a concentrated, delicious taste that you only need a small spoonful to boost the flavor of any dish. I've enjoyed shallot marmalade on grilled cheese, hummus or avocado toast, cheese boards, portabella mushroom caps, and veggie burgers. The opportunities for this game-changing recipe are endless.*

**2 tablespoons extra-virgin olive oil**

**2 pounds shallots, thinly sliced**

**1 tablespoon fresh thyme leaves**

**½ cup balsamic vinegar**

**3 tablespoons light brown sugar**

1. In a large skillet, warm the olive oil over medium heat.

2. Add the shallots and thyme. Cook for about 10 minutes, or until tender.

3. Add the vinegar and sugar. Cook for 10 minutes, or until the liquid has mostly evaporated and the shallots are caramelized and sticky. Remove from the heat.

**NOTE:** Store in a glass jar or airtight container in the refrigerator for up to 1 week.

# Spinach

**Season:** spring, fall

**Flavor profile:** Spinach has a grassy, earthy taste that's milder than peppery arugula or hearty kale. It is not as tough as some leafy greens, making it an ideal base for salads.

**Pairs with:** olive oil, most vinegars, cheeses, garlic, soy sauce, ginger, red pepper flakes, artichokes, most fresh fruits

**Varieties:** baby or mature flat-leaf, curly-leaf (known as savoy or semi-savoy)

**Preparation:** Rinse clean in a colander under cold water. Pat dry or use a salad spinner to get rid of excess water.

Spinach can be chopped with a chef's knife or in a food processor.

**Favorite ways to serve:** raw in salads, blended into smoothies, sautéed

**Nutritional info:** Not only is spinach a source of iron, calcium, folate, and vitamins A, C, and K, but also it's loaded with antioxidants such as quercetin and kaempferol.

**Selection:** Fresh spinach is bright green and crisp. Avoid spinach with leaves that are yellowed, wilted, or look slimy.

**Storage:** Wrap unwashed spinach in paper towels to help absorb moisture and prolong its shelf life. Store in a plastic bag or in its original container for up to five days in the refrigerator.

# Easy Wilted Spinach

**SERVES 4** / **PREP TIME:** 5 minutes / **COOK TIME:** 5 minutes

1 tablespoon extra-virgin
    olive oil

3 garlic cloves, minced

8 cups loosely
    packed spinach

Salt

Freshly ground
    black pepper

4 lemon wedges (optional)

1. In a large skillet, warm the olive oil over medium heat.

2. Add the garlic, and cook for 3 to 4 minutes, or until fragrant.

3. Add the spinach, and cook for 3 to 5 minutes, or until wilted. Season with salt and pepper to taste. Remove from the heat.

4. Sprinkle the spinach with lemon juice just before serving (if using).

# Everyday Spinach Salad

**SERVES 4 TO 6 / PREP TIME:** 15 minutes

*When I have no idea what to throw together for lunch, a spinach salad never fails me. I start with fresh spinach, then add other vegetables I have on hand, nuts or seeds, a source of lean protein, and dried fruit. This recipe is my favorite rendition of spinach salad. It's filling, nutritious, and energizing enough to power me through a busy afternoon.*

**6 cups loosely packed coarsely chopped spinach**

**4 hard-boiled eggs, peeled and sliced**

**2 carrots, sliced**

**1 ripe avocado, pitted, peeled, and sliced**

**1 cup shredded vegetarian mozzarella cheese**

**½ cup pistachios**

**½ cup dried cherries**

**Shallot-Dijon Vinaigrette** (page 233)

1. In a large bowl, toss together the spinach, eggs, carrots, avocado, mozzarella cheese, pistachios, and dried cherries.

2. Add the vinaigrette and toss until evenly coated.

**NOTE:** To make this vegan, omit the cheese and substitute beans for the eggs.

# Spinach and White Bean Stir-Fry

**SERVES 4** / **PREP TIME:** 5 minutes / **COOK TIME:** 15 minutes

*Since sautéed spinach cooks down quickly, you can pack a ton of this nutritious green into stir-fries. With a touch of coconut milk, spicy red pepper flakes, creamy white beans, and chewy farro, eating your greens has never been this delicious. Bookmark this easy vegetarian main dish for when you have a hankering for a fast meal that's still healthy and tasty.*

**1 tablespoon extra-virgin olive oil**

**3 garlic cloves, minced**

**8 cups loosely packed spinach**

**¼ cup full-fat plain coconut milk**

**1 tablespoon soy sauce**

**⅛ to ¼ teaspoon red pepper flakes**

**1 (15-ounce) can white beans, drained and rinsed**

**2 cups cooked farro**

1. In a large skillet, warm the olive oil over medium heat.

2. Add the garlic and cook for 3 to 4 minutes, or until fragrant.

3. Add the spinach, coconut milk, soy sauce, and red pepper flakes. Stir to combine. Cook for 3 to 5 minutes, or until the spinach has wilted.

4. Add the beans and cook for 3 to 4 minutes, or until warmed through. Remove from the heat.

5. Divide the farro among 4 shallow bowls. Top with the spinach mixture and spoon any remaining sauce on top before serving.

**NOTE:** Prep the farro in advance to have on hand for when you make this dish. You can find quick-cooking farro at Trader Joe's and some other stores.

# Peaches and "Cream" Spinach Smoothie

**SERVES 4** / **PREP TIME:** 5 minutes

*The mild taste of spinach makes it one of the best greens to use in smoothies. You can't go wrong with a combination of spinach and any frozen fruit, but I especially enjoy this play on peaches and cream. Make this indulgent yet healthy treat to refuel after exercise, for breakfast, or as an after-school snack for the kids.*

**2 cups loosely packed spinach**

**1½ cups frozen sliced peaches**

**1 cup full-fat plain coconut milk**

**¼ cup old-fashioned oats**

**1 teaspoon maple syrup, plus more as needed**

**Dash vanilla extract**

In a blender, combine the spinach, peaches, coconut milk, oats, maple syrup, vanilla, and 1 cup of water. Blend until smooth. Taste, and add more maple syrup as needed.

NOTE: Swap in 1 or 2 pitted dates for the maple syrup to sweeten the smoothie.

# Open-Face Spinach and Artichoke Melts

**SERVES 4** / **PREP TIME:** 15 minutes / **COOK TIME:** 5 minutes

*These plant-based melts capture the distinct flavors of spinach-artichoke dip, with hints of creamy ricotta, garlic, feta, and parmesan in every bite. For maximum flavor, use Marinated Artichoke Hearts (page 13) instead of plain ones. Either way, this recipe is definitely one to come back to again and again when you need an easy, warm meal.*

**4 large bread slices, toasted**

**1 cup whole-milk vegetarian ricotta cheese**

**2 garlic cloves, minced**

**1½ cups chopped spinach**

**¼ cup crumbled vegetarian feta cheese**

**Salt**

**Freshly ground black pepper**

**8 to 10 artichoke hearts, quartered**

**½ cup freshly grated vegetarian Parmesan cheese**

1. Turn the broiler to high. Line a baking sheet with aluminum foil. Put the bread on the prepared baking sheet.

2. In a bowl, mix together the ricotta cheese, garlic, spinach, and feta cheese. Season with salt and pepper.

3. Spread the ricotta mixture onto the bread slices.

4. Add the artichoke hearts and parmesan cheese on top.

5. Transfer the baking sheet to the oven and broil for 3 to 4 minutes, or until the cheese has melted. Remove from the oven.

**NOTE:** You can make the spinach-ricotta spread up to 4 days ahead and store in an airtight container in the refrigerator.

# Sweet Potatoes

**Season:** fall, winter

**Flavor profile:** As their name suggests, sweet potatoes have a deliciously sweet taste that's reminiscent of some winter squashes. When cooked, they have creamy flesh and buttery mouthfeel.

**Pairs with:** butter, rosemary, sage, cinnamon, ginger, coconut, chili powder, paprika, apples, onions, walnuts, pecans

**Varieties:** orange, yellow, red, white, or purple skin with orange, yellow, white, or purple flesh

**Preparation:** Scrub clean with a vegetable brush, and use a swivel peeler to remove the skin if desired. Roast whole or dice.

**Favorite ways to serve:** roasted, mashed, stuffed, made into noodles

**Nutritional info:** Sweet potatoes are known for being an extremely good source of beta-carotene, the pigment that's responsible for their orange flesh and gets converted to vitamin A in the body. Consuming enough vitamin A is vital to maintaining good eyesight.

**Selection:** Choose firm sweet potatoes with smooth skin that's not cracked. Small or medium sweet potatoes tend to be sweeter than larger ones.

**Storage:** Keep sweet potatoes in a cool, dry, and dark place. Use within two weeks.

# Roasted Sweet Potatoes

**SERVES 4 TO 6 / PREP TIME:** 5 minutes / **COOK TIME:** 40 minutes

**4 sweet potatoes, diced**

**2 tablespoons extra-virgin olive oil**

**Salt**

1. Preheat the oven to 400°F. Line a baking sheet with parchment paper.

2. On the prepared baking sheet, toss the sweet potatoes with the olive oil until evenly coated.

3. Arrange the sweet potatoes in a single layer. Season with salt.

4. Transfer the baking sheet to the oven and roast for 30 to 40 minutes, flipping halfway through, or until the sweet potatoes are tender and browned. Remove from the oven.

**NOTE:** For a spicy kick, sprinkle the sweet potatoes with 1 teaspoon chili powder before roasting. For a sweeter seasoning, toss the potatoes in 2 tablespoons melted butter with 1 tablespoon light brown sugar and ½ teaspoon ground cinnamon.

# Stuffed Sweet Potatoes with Pesto and White Beans

**SERVES 4** / **PREP TIME:** 5 minutes / **COOK TIME:** 50 minutes

*When I was growing up, my mom often prepared baked potatoes for dinner but would make a sweet potato for herself. It wasn't until I was an adult and got over my childhood aversions to sweet potatoes that I realized she was onto something. Baked sweet potatoes are creamy and delicious and have the most beautifully colored flesh. As a rich source of complex carbohydrates, vitamins, and minerals, they make for a supremely healthy base for a quick dinner.*

**4 sweet potatoes**

**1 cup Sunflower Seed and Arugula Pesto** (page 20)

**1 (15-ounce) can white beans, drained and rinsed**

1. Preheat the oven to 425°F. Place a sheet of aluminum foil on the center rack of the oven.

2. Using a fork, poke several holes in the skin of the sweet potatoes. Place on the foil and roast for 40 to 50 minutes, or until soft and cooked through. Remove from the oven.

3. While the sweet potatoes cook, in a medium bowl, toss the pesto and beans together, and let marinate.

4. Cut the sweet potatoes open lengthwise, and fluff the flesh with a fork.

5. Add a generous scoop of the pesto beans. Enjoy immediately, or return the sweet potatoes to the oven to heat for a few more minutes.

**NOTE:** You can use any pesto for this recipe or the Homemade Chimichurri (page 151) for a vegan option.

# Sweet Potato and Chickpea Curry

**SERVES 4** / **PREP TIME:** 10 minutes / **COOK TIME:** 25 minutes

*Curry is the best kind of vegetarian meal: full of flavor and so easy to prepare. In this version, tender sweet potatoes are simmered in a luscious coconut-based sauce. Enjoy this comforting meal for dinner on a cold night and have the leftovers for lunch the next day . . . or not. I have a feeling you'll be hurrying back for seconds with this one.*

**2 tablespoons coconut oil**

**1 yellow onion, diced**

**3 garlic cloves, minced**

**1 sweet potato, diced**

**2 teaspoons curry powder**

**1 teaspoon ground cumin**

**½ teaspoon ground ginger**

**2 cups vegetable broth**

**1 (13½-ounce) can full-fat coconut milk**

**1 (15-ounce) can chickpeas, drained and rinsed**

1. In a large skillet, warm the coconut oil over medium heat.

2. Add the onion and garlic. Cook for 3 to 4 minutes, or until fragrant.

3. Add the sweet potato, curry powder, cumin, ground ginger, and broth. Stir to combine.

4. Reduce the heat to medium-low. Cover and simmer for about 10 minutes, or until the sweet potato is almost tender.

5. Add the coconut milk and chickpeas.

6. Increase the heat to medium. Cook, uncovered, stirring occasionally, for 8 to 10 minutes, or until the curry begins to thicken. Remove from the heat. Serve warm.

**NOTE:** Enjoy this curry on its own, with naan bread, or with rice. Use curry paste in lieu of curry powder for an even spicier dish.

# Rosemary Mashed Sweet Potatoes

**SERVES 6** / **PREP TIME:** 10 minutes / **COOK TIME:** 20 minutes

*The velvety smooth texture of cooked sweet potatoes lends itself to a variety of culinary uses, especially a basic mash. Although this dish may have fewer ingredients than my classic mashed potatoes, it certainly does not lack in flavor. Serve it on the side with cauliflower steaks or as a base for baked beans. The sweet-savory undertones go well with all sorts of entrées.*

**2 pounds sweet potatoes, peeled and cut into chunks**

**3 tablespoons melted salted butter**

**1 tablespoon chopped fresh rosemary**

**Salt**

1. Put the sweet potatoes in a large pot, cover with water, and bring to a boil over high heat.

2. Reduce the heat to a simmer. Cook for 12 to 15 minutes, or until the sweet potatoes are fork-tender. Remove from the heat. Drain and return to the pot.

3. Add the butter and rosemary. Season with salt. Using a hand mixer, whip the sweet potatoes until smooth. For a chunkier texture, use a potato masher.

**NOTE:** For a seasonal topping, add rosemary-thyme pecans (see page 75). To make this recipe vegan, use olive oil instead of butter.

# Egg and Spiralized Sweet Potato Skillet

**SERVES 4 / PREP TIME:** 10 minutes / **COOK TIME:** 20 minutes

*This meal is on regular rotation in our household, especially after a long day, when what to make for dinner is the last thing on my mind. My husband and I came up with this dish one evening when our refrigerator was mostly bare except for a few basics and a sweet potato. It was so yummy and easy to make that we still make it years later. I hope it becomes that kind of recipe for you.*

**3 tablespoons coconut oil**

**2 sweet potatoes, spiralized into noodles**

**Salt**

**Freshly ground black pepper**

**4 large eggs**

1. In a large cast-iron or other oven-safe skillet, warm the coconut oil over medium heat.

2. Add the sweet potatoes and cook, stirring occasionally, for about 15 minutes, or until tender. The pan will be overcrowded at first until the sweet potatoes cook down. Season with salt and pepper. Remove from the heat.

3. Turn the broiler to high.

4. Using a spoon, shift around the noodles to make 4 wells.

5. Carefully crack an egg into each well.

6. Using an oven mitt, transfer the skillet to the oven, and broil for 3 to 5 minutes, or until the eggs are cooked to your liking. Remove from the oven. Serve warm.

**NOTE:** Possible additions include crumbled vegetarian feta or goat cheese and chopped fresh parsley or cilantro. To make the noodles easier to eat, snip them into smaller pieces with kitchen scissors before cooking.

# Tomatoes

**Season:** summer

**Flavor profile:** Even though they are technically considered fruits, tomatoes are often grouped with vegetables for culinary purposes. They have juicy flesh and a sweet, acidic taste that's slightly different for each variety.

**Pairs with:** garlic, onion, olive oil, mozzarella cheese, basil, thyme, chives, parsley, cilantro, red pepper flakes, stone fruits

**Varieties:** beefsteak, heirloom, San Marzano, cherry, grape, and several other varieties that can be red, green, or yellow-orange

**Preparation:** Remove the stems, wash, and pat dry. Use a serrated knife to cut tomatoes.

**Favorite ways to serve:** raw, grilled, blended into sauce or soups

**Nutritional info:** Tomatoes provide a variety of nutrients and health-promoting compounds, including the red pigment lycopene. This antioxidant may help lower blood pressure and prevent the buildup of plaque in arteries.

**Selection:** Look for tomatoes that are plump, smooth, and free of cracks or dark spots. To truly test their freshness, pick up tomatoes and smell them to ensure that they have a sweet, earthy fragrance.

**Storage:** Put ripe or almost ripe tomatoes on a plate, and store at room temperature away from direct sunlight for a few days. Overripe tomatoes can be refrigerated to prevent rotting but should be used within two days.

# Tomato Caprese Salad

**SERVES 4 TO 6 / PREP TIME:** 5 minutes

4 heirloom
tomatoes, sliced

1 (8-ounce) ball
fresh vegetarian
mozzarella, sliced

6 to 8 fresh basil leaves,
coarsely torn

2 tablespoons extra-virgin
olive oil

Salt

Freshly ground
black pepper

1. Arrange the tomatoes, mozzarella cheese, and basil on a plate or serving dish.

2. Drizzle the olive oil on top. Season with salt and pepper.

NOTE: Other delicious additions include a drizzle of balsamic vinegar or balsamic reduction and fresh peaches, nectarines, berries, cantaloupe, or other types of seasonal fruit.

# Grilled Tomatoes with Homemade Chimichurri

**SERVES 4** / **PREP TIME:** 10 minutes / **COOK TIME:** 10 minutes

*The intersection of grilling season with peak tomato harvest is a magical time for home chefs. Grilled tomatoes pack a punch of sweetness, a little bit of smokiness, and a jammy texture. If you usually eat tomatoes raw, I encourage you to give this recipe a try. A light char is all you need to take tomatoes to the next level.*

**8 roma tomatoes,
   halved lengthwise**
**1 tablespoon extra-virgin
   olive oil**
**Salt**
**Freshly ground
   black pepper**
**Homemade Chimichurri**
   (page 151)

1. Preheat the grill on medium-high heat.

2. Using a spoon or your hands, remove and discard the pulp from the tomatoes. Transfer the tomatoes to a bowl.

3. Add the olive oil and toss. Season with salt and pepper.

4. Place the tomatoes, cut-side down, on the grill or on a vegetable mat on the grill. Cook for 3 to 4 minutes on each side, or until tender and lightly charred. Remove from the heat. Transfer to a serving dish.

5. Spoon chimichurri on top and serve.

**NOTE:** You can use other varieties of tomatoes for this recipe, but make sure they are big enough to keep their shape on the grill and won't slip through the cracks.

# Homemade Tomato Sauce

**MAKES ABOUT 3 CUPS** / **PREP TIME:** 5 minutes / **COOK TIME:** 20 to 25 minutes

*Making tomato sauce from scratch may sound intimidating, but as soon as you see how easy it is, you'll wonder why you didn't try it sooner. The key to a truly delicious sauce is using San Marzano tomatoes, which are known for their sweetness and low acidity. Once you have the proper ingredients, the stovetop does the rest of the work. If you go through a lot of tomato sauce in your house, I recommend making this recipe in bulk and freezing for later.*

2 tablespoons extra-virgin
  olive oil

4 garlic cloves, minced

1 (28-ounce) can
  whole peeled San
  Marzano tomatoes

½ teaspoon salt, plus
  more as needed

Freshly ground
  black pepper

1. In a saucepan, warm the olive oil and garlic over medium-low heat. Cook for 2 to 3 minutes, stirring frequently to avoid burning, or until fragrant.

2. Add the tomatoes along with their juices and the salt. Simmer, using a wooden spoon to crush the tomatoes as they cook, for 15 to 20 minutes, or until the sauce has reached your desired thickness. Season with salt and pepper to taste. Remove from the heat.

**NOTE:** Use this sauce immediately, or transfer to glass jars, let cool, and store in the refrigerator for up to 1 week. To freeze, let cool to room temperature before transferring to freezer-safe containers. It will last for at least 3 months in the freezer. Thaw in the refrigerator before using. To make this more like a marinara sauce, add up to 1 teaspoon each of dried basil and oregano and a pinch of red pepper flakes for some spice.

# Spicy Tomato Jam

**MAKES ABOUT 2 CUPS / PREP TIME:** 15 minutes / **COOK TIME:** 55 minutes to 1 hour

*Turning tomatoes into jam is a great way to extend their season well into the fall. This versatile condiment is a killer addition to a cheese board and doubles as a tasty spread for toast, biscuits, or bagels with cream cheese. A teaspoon of red pepper flakes yields a mildly spicy jam, so adjust the amount you use depending on how spicy you want it.*

**3 pounds plum tomatoes, cored and cut into 1-inch pieces**

**½ cup maple syrup**

**1 teaspoon smoked paprika**

**1 to 2 teaspoons red pepper flakes**

**½ teaspoon salt, plus more as needed**

1. In a saucepan, combine the tomatoes, maple syrup, paprika, red pepper flakes, and salt. Bring to a rapid simmer over medium heat, stirring frequently to prevent scorching.

2. Reduce the heat to medium-low. Cook, stirring occasionally, for 45 to 55 minutes, or until the jam begins to thicken and most of the juices have evaporated. Remove from the heat. Transfer to a glass jar and let cool.

**NOTE:** Tomato jam keeps in the refrigerator for up to 2 weeks.

# Garden Tomato Soup with Cheddar Toasties

**SERVES 4 TO 6** / **PREP TIME:** 15 minutes / **COOK TIME:** 25 to 30 minutes

*If there were ever a recipe for your late summer garden overflowing with tomatoes, it's this one. Instead of canned tomatoes, I like to throw in the freshest, juiciest tomatoes I can find in my backyard or at the farmers' market. If you don't own an immersion blender, see page 27 for notes on making this in a regular blender.*

## FOR THE SOUP

- 2 tablespoons extra-virgin olive oil
- 1 sweet onion, diced
- 3 garlic cloves, minced
- 4 cups chopped fresh tomatoes with their juices, any variety
- 1 teaspoon tomato paste
- 2 cups vegetable broth
- ½ teaspoon salt, plus more as needed
- ¼ teaspoon freshly ground black pepper, plus more as needed

## FOR THE TOASTIES

- 12 thin baguette slices
- ½ cup freshly shredded vegetarian cheddar cheese
- 1 to 2 tablespoons chiffonade fresh basil

## TO MAKE THE SOUP

1. In a large pot or Dutch oven, warm the olive oil over medium heat.

2. Add the onion and garlic. Cook for 3 to 4 minutes, or until fragrant.

3. Add the tomatoes and tomato paste. Cook for 5 to 7 minutes, or until the tomatoes start to break down and become tender.

4. Add the broth, salt, and pepper. Simmer for about 15 minutes, or until the tomatoes have completely broken down. Remove from the heat.

5. Using an immersion blender, puree the soup in the pot. Season with salt and pepper to taste.

## TO MAKE THE TOASTIES

6. Turn the broiler to high.

7. On a baking sheet, sprinkle the baguette slices with the cheddar cheese.

8. Transfer the baking sheet to the oven and broil for 1 to 2 minutes, or until the cheese has just melted. Remove from the oven.

9. Sprinkle the basil on top of the soup. Serve warm with a few toasties on the side.

# Turnips

**Season:** fall, winter

**Flavor profile:** Turnips are a crunchy root vegetable with a pungent taste that's mildly bitter and spicy. Cooking helps to mellow their flavor, and younger turnips are generally sweeter than more mature ones. Turnip greens are also edible and taste similar to the roots.

**Pairs with:** butter, cream, mustard, sage, rosemary, chives, thyme, garlic, apples, carrots, beets, potatoes, gruyère cheese

**Varieties:** purple-top, baby, all-white, scarlet

**Preparation:** Scrub clean with a vegetable brush, peel if desired, and dice.

**Favorite ways to serve:** grated, shaved, roasted, mashed, made into noodles

**Nutritional info:** Turnips are part of the cruciferous vegetable family and may provide similar health benefits as kale, Brussels sprouts, and bok choy. They are rich in both vitamin C and glucosinolates, compounds that may prevent cancer cell growth.

**Selection:** Turnips should be firm and heavy. Their skin should be smooth and free of cracks.

**Storage:** Keep whole, unwashed turnips in a plastic bag or airtight container in the refrigerator for two weeks or longer.

# Maple-Mustard Roasted Turnips

**SERVES 4 / PREP TIME:** 5 minutes / **COOK TIME:** 35 minutes

2 tablespoons
   maple syrup
1 tablespoon
   Dijon mustard
1 tablespoon extra-virgin
   olive oil
2 large turnips, peeled
   and diced
Salt
Chopped fresh
   parsley or thyme, for
   serving (optional)

1. Preheat the oven to 400°F. Line a baking sheet with parchment paper.

2. In a medium bowl, stir together the maple syrup, mustard, and olive oil.

3. Add the turnips, and toss until evenly coated.

4. Spread the turnips out in a single layer on the prepared baking sheet. Season with salt to taste.

5. Transfer the baking sheet to the oven, and roast for 30 to 35 minutes, flipping halfway through, or until the turnips are tender. Remove from the oven.

6. Garnish the turnips with fresh parsley or thyme (if using).

# Pureed Turnip and Garlic Dip

**MAKES ABOUT 3 CUPS** / **PREP TIME:** 10 minutes / **COOK TIME:** 30 minutes

*Roasting root vegetables brings out their natural sweetness, and roasted turnips are no exception. Turnips also take on a tender, buttery texture when cooked, making them an ideal base for creamy dips. This healthy snack pairs mellowed turnips with roasted garlic. It's zesty, nutritious, and a great companion to seed crackers or tortilla chips.*

**3 cups diced turnips**

**3 tablespoons extra-virgin olive oil, divided**

**Salt**

**Freshly ground black pepper**

**3 to 4 cloves from Roasted Garlic Bulbs** (page 133)

**Juice of ½ lemon**

**Toasted sesame seeds, for topping**

1. Preheat the oven to 400°F. Line a baking sheet with parchment paper.

2. On the prepared baking sheet, toss the turnips with 1 tablespoon of olive oil. Season with salt and pepper.

3. Transfer the baking sheet to the oven and bake for about 30 minutes, or until the turnips are tender. Remove from the oven.

4. In a food processor or high-powered blender, combine the turnips, garlic, lemon juice, and remaining 2 tablespoons of olive oil. Season with salt and pepper. Pulse until smooth. Season with salt and pepper to taste. Transfer to a serving bowl.

5. Top the dip with toasted sesame seeds.

**NOTE:** Although cloves from a whole roasted garlic bulb add more creamy texture and flavor, you can also roast the individual garlic cloves with the turnips if you're short on time. Store the dip for up to one week in an airtight container in the refrigerator.

# Apple, Carrot, and Turnip Slaw

**SERVES 4 TO 6 / PREP TIME:** 15 minutes

*Move over coleslaw, there's a new veggie slaw in town, and it's here to stay. This crunchy dish has sweet hints from apple, carrots, and an apple cider vinegar dressing and a slightly peppery bite from raw turnip. Though this combo tastes delicious no matter how it's prepared, if you have a julienne peeler or the patience to julienne vegetables with a knife, it's worth taking the few extra minutes to make the vegetables thin and stringy like in a true slaw.*

**FOR THE DRESSING**

¼ cup extra-virgin olive oil

3 tablespoons apple cider vinegar

1 tablespoon honey

½ teaspoon salt

**FOR THE SLAW**

2 carrots, julienned or coarsely grated

1 large apple, peeled and julienned or coarsely grated

1 turnip, peeled and julienned or coarsely grated

2 to 3 tablespoons chopped fresh parsley

Salt

**TO MAKE THE DRESSING**

1. In a large bowl, whisk together the olive oil, vinegar, honey, and salt.

**TO MAKE THE SLAW**

2. Add the carrots, apple, and turnip.

3. Sprinkle the parsley on top. Toss until evenly coated. Season with salt to taste.

**NOTE:** I like to use Pink Lady apples for this slaw, but you can also use Granny Smith for a tarter flavor. If the salad is slightly bitter for your liking, add a dash more cider vinegar and up to 1 teaspoon sugar. You can also substitute fresh mint for the parsley. This salad keeps well in the refrigerator for up to 3 days, but the apples will brown over time.

# Peanut-Ginger Turnip Noodles

**SERVES 4 TO 6** / **PREP TIME:** 15 minutes / **COOK TIME:** 20 to 25 minutes

*Spiralized turnips stand in for rice noodles in this Thai-inspired dish. The turnips are cooked until tender, mixed with crunchy vegetable toppings, and smothered in a creamy, five-ingredient peanut-ginger sauce. After trying this dish, you'll be counting down the days until you see turnips again at the market or in your CSA share.*

## FOR THE SAUCE

2 tablespoons soy sauce

2 tablespoons creamy peanut butter

Juice of ½ lime

1 tablespoon honey

2 teaspoons finely chopped fresh ginger

## FOR THE VEGETABLES

1 tablespoon extra-virgin olive oil

3 garlic cloves, minced

2 turnips, spiralized into noodles

1 cup sugar snap peas

1 bell pepper, seeded and diced

2 carrots, sliced

4 scallions, green and white parts, thinly sliced

½ cup chopped peanuts

## TO MAKE THE SAUCE

1. In a small bowl, whisk together the soy sauce, peanut butter, lime juice, honey, and ginger.

## TO MAKE THE VEGETABLES

2. In a large skillet, warm the olive oil over medium heat.

3. Add the garlic, and cook for 3 to 4 minutes, or until fragrant.

4. Add the turnips, and cook, stirring occasionally, for 6 to 8 minutes, or until tender but still slightly crunchy.

5. Add the snap peas, bell pepper, and carrots. Cook for 6 to 8 minutes, or until the vegetables have softened.

6. Add the sauce. Stir until the vegetables are evenly coated. Cook for 3 to 4 minutes, or until warmed through. Remove from the heat.

7. Serve the vegetables with the scallions and peanuts.

**NOTE:** Use tamari in place of soy sauce to make this dish gluten-free and maple syrup in place of honey to make it vegan. Possible additions include cooked edamame or tofu.

# Watercress

**Season:** spring

**Flavor profile:** Watercress is named as such because it grows in permanently wet soil or submerged in water. A relative of horseradish, it has a strong peppery taste that's similar to arugula. It's often used as a garnish or herb but can also stand alone as the main ingredient in recipes.

**Pairs with:** olive oil, lemon, red wine vinegar, berries, oranges, honey, shallots, garlic, cashews, pistachios

**Varieties:** several, all with thin stems and small leaves

**Preparation:** Use a sharp knife to cut off the tough ends of the stems. Discard any yellow leaves. Submerge the watercress in a bowl with cold water, and use your hands to gently swish away any dirt. Pat dry with a clean towel.

**Favorite ways to serve:** as a garnish, raw in salads, used in place of herbs in pesto

**Nutritional info:** Watercress has very few calories but significant amounts of vitamin K, a bone-strengthening nutrient that also helps with blood clotting.

**Selection:** Choose watercress that has bright green, strong leaves that are not yellow, slimy, or wilted.

**Storage:** Store watercress upright, with its stems submerged in a jar of water and its leaves loosely covered with a plastic bag, for up to five days in the refrigerator.

# Watercress and Goat Cheese Salad with Strawberry Tahini

**SERVES 4 / PREP TIME:** 5 minutes

## FOR THE STRAWBERRY-TAHINI DRESSING

**3 tablespoons tahini**
**1 cup fresh strawberries**
**Juice of ½ lemon**
**Salt**

## FOR THE SALAD

**2 bunches watercress, trimmed**
**½ cup crumbled vegetarian goat cheese**
**½ cup chopped red onion**

## TO MAKE THE STRAWBERRY-TAHINI DRESSING

1. In a blender or food processor, combine the tahini, strawberries, and lemon juice. Pulse until smooth, drizzling water through the hole at the top as needed to thin the dressing. Season with salt to taste.

## TO MAKE THE SALAD

2. Arrange the watercress on serving plates, drizzle with the dressing, and sprinkle the goat cheese and onion on top.

# Watercress and Toasted Cashew Pesto

**MAKES ABOUT 2 CUPS / PREP TIME:** 10 minutes / **COOK TIME:** 5 minutes

*Since the tiny leaves of watercress pack a strong flavor, they can take the place of fresh herbs in recipes. This nontraditional pesto uses watercress in place of basil and toasted cashews instead of pine nuts. I enjoy it as a dipping sauce for sliced carrots, tossed with pasta, spread on toast topped with an egg, or as the base for a spring-inspired pizza.*

**½ cup raw cashews**

**4 cups loosely packed watercress leaves**

**1 garlic clove, minced**

**½ cup freshly grated vegetarian parmesan cheese**

**Juice of ½ lemon**

**⅓ cup olive oil, plus more as needed**

**Salt**

1. In a skillet, toast the cashews over medium heat for 3 to 5 minutes, or until fragrant. Remove from the heat.

2. In a food processor or high-powered blender, combine the cashews, watercress, garlic, parmesan cheese, and lemon juice.

3. Pour in the olive oil and pulse until smooth. Stop to scrape down the sides with a rubber spatula, and add more olive oil as needed. Season with salt to taste.

**NOTE:** Store in a glass jar or airtight container in the refrigerator for up to 1 week. You can also freeze this pesto for at least 3 months or sometimes longer.

# Winter Squash

**Season:** fall, winter

**Flavor profile:** From the sweet flavor of butternut to the earthy, nutty palate of acorn, winter squashes vary in taste. In general, the flesh of cooked squash is rich and creamy with subtly sweet undertones.

**Pairs with:** butter, rosemary, sage, thyme, cinnamon, cloves, allspice, nutmeg, ginger, apples, pears, cranberries

**Varieties:** acorn, butternut, delicata, Hubbard, kabocha, pumpkin, red kuri, spaghetti

**Preparation:** Use a chef's knife to remove the top and stem. Cut in half lengthwise from top to bottom, scoop out the seeds with a spoon, and remove the skin with a swivel peeler or knife. Cut into desired shapes. If the squash is difficult to cut, make several slits with a knife on the part of the skin where you want to cut it in half. Microwave on high for 3 to 4 minutes to soften the skin.

**Favorite ways to serve:** roasted, stuffed, pureed

**Nutritional info:** The nutrition of each type of winter squash varies, but they are all rich in fiber and micronutrients. Most squashes provide generous amounts of antioxidant carotenoids that are responsible for their bright-colored flesh.

**Selection:** Pick up the squash to ensure that it feels heavy and has a smooth surface without cracks or bruises. Squash stems should be dry and firm.

**Storage:** Winter squash will keep for at least a few weeks when stored in a cool, dry place.

# Roasted Winter Squash

**SERVES 4 TO 6 / PREP TIME:** 10 minutes / **COOK TIME:** 40 minutes

1 winter squash, peeled,
   seeded, and diced
1 tablespoon extra-virgin
   olive oil
Salt
Freshly ground
   black pepper

1. Preheat the oven to 400°F. Line a baking sheet with parchment paper.

2. On the prepared baking sheet, toss the squash with the olive oil. Season with salt and pepper.

3. Transfer the baking sheet to the oven and roast for 30 to 40 minutes, or until the squash is tender. Remove from the oven.

NOTE: For a sweet variation, toss the squash in 1 tablespoon each olive oil and maple syrup and ½ teaspoon ground cinnamon. Add a pinch of cayenne pepper for some spice.

# Delicata Squash Eggs-in-a-Hole

**SERVES 4** / **PREP TIME:** 10 minutes / **COOK TIME:** 25 minutes

*Squash is usually thought of as a classic side dish for a fall or winter dinner, but it also shines at the breakfast table. Delicata squash rings, in particular, have perfectly shaped hollow centers for making eggs-in-a-hole. Dress up this simple but elegant autumnal dish with sage brown butter (see page 267), fresh rosemary or thyme, creamy goat cheese, or chopped pecans.*

**1 delicata squash,
seeded and cut into
1-inch-thick slices**

**1 teaspoon extra-virgin
olive oil**

**Salt**

**Freshly ground
black pepper**

**4 large eggs, plus
more as needed to fill
the rings**

1. Preheat the oven to 400°F. Line a baking sheet with parchment paper.

2. On the prepared baking sheet, brush the squash rings on both sides with the olive oil.

3. Arrange the squash in a single layer. Season with salt and pepper.

4. Transfer the baking sheet to the oven and roast for 15 minutes, or until the squash is slightly tender. Remove from the oven.

5. Reduce the oven temperature to 350°F.

6. Carefully crack 1 egg into each squash ring.

7. Return the baking sheet to the oven and bake for 8 to 10 minutes, or until the eggs are cooked to your desired consistency. Remove from the oven.

**NOTE:** Use a large delicata squash to get the most rings. Serve with a side salad or fresh fruit.

# Butternut Squash Soup with Caramelized Pears

**SERVES 4 TO 6** / **PREP TIME:** 15 minutes / **COOK TIME:** 35 minutes

*A classic butternut squash soup recipe should be in every home cook's arsenal. The silky texture of butternut makes for a rich soup that needs just a few other ingredients to come together. I love cozying up under a blanket with a warm bowl of this in my hands on the first chilly day of the year. And thanks to a topping of caramelized pears, it's also fit for a holiday meal or sit-down dinner.*

## FOR THE CARAMELIZED PEARS

**2 tablespoons unsalted butter**

**4 small pears, finely diced**

**2 tablespoons light brown sugar**

**½ teaspoon ground cinnamon**

## FOR THE SOUP

**2 tablespoons unsalted butter**

**1 yellow onion, diced**

**½ teaspoon salt, plus more as needed**

**1 butternut squash, peeled, seeded, and cut into 1-inch chunks**

**1 teaspoon chopped fresh thyme leaves**

**4 cups vegetable broth**

**Freshly ground black pepper**

### TO MAKE THE CARAMELIZED PEARS

1. In a skillet, melt the butter over medium heat.

2. Add the pears, sugar, and cinnamon. Cook for 10 minutes, flipping halfway through, or until soft and caramelized. Remove from the heat.

### TO MAKE THE SOUP

3. Meanwhile, in a large soup pot, melt the butter over medium heat.

4. Stir in the onion and salt. Cook for 3 to 4 minutes, or until softened.

5. Add the squash, thyme, and broth. Season with salt and pepper to taste. Bring to a boil.

6. Reduce the heat to medium-low. Simmer for 25 to 30 minutes, or until the squash is tender. Remove from the heat.

7. Using an immersion blender, puree the soup in the pot.

8. Serve the soup warm with the caramelized pears on top.

**NOTE:** For an even creamier soup, stir in ½ cup heavy cream before blending.

# Spaghetti Squash Noodles with Sage Brown Butter

**SERVES 4 TO 6** / **PREP TIME:** 10 minutes / **COOK TIME:** 40 minutes

*At first glance, the inside of a spaghetti squash looks similar to other squash varieties. But as its name suggests, cooking transforms the flesh of this unique vegetable into yummy noodles. Spaghetti squash doesn't actually taste like pasta, but it's delicious in its own right and great at soaking up flavors. Try it with a simple brown butter sauce for a meal that will knock your socks off. The cooking time will vary depending on the size of the squash.*

**FOR THE SPAGHETTI SQUASH**

**1 spaghetti squash, halved and seeded**
**1 teaspoon olive oil, for brushing**
**Salt**
**Freshly ground black pepper**

**FOR THE SAGE BROWN BUTTER**

**8 tablespoons (1 stick) unsalted butter**
**¼ cup chopped fresh sage, plus more as needed**
**1 to 2 teaspoons grated lemon zest**
**Freshly ground black pepper**
**½ cup toasted pine nuts**

**TO MAKE THE SPAGHETTI SQUASH**

1. Preheat the oven to 400°F. Line a baking sheet with parchment paper.

2. Brush the cut sides of the spaghetti squash with the olive oil. Sprinkle with salt and pepper.

3. Place the squash, cut-sides down, on the prepared baking sheet.

4. Transfer the baking sheet to the oven, and roast for 30 to 40 minutes, or until the squash is tender and you can pull the flesh away with a fork. Remove from the oven.

**TO MAKE THE SAGE BROWN BUTTER**

5. A few minutes before the squash has finished cooking, in a small saucepan, melt the butter over medium-low heat.

6. Add the sage and lemon zest. Season with pepper. Simmer for 3 to 4 minutes, or until the butter has lightly browned. Remove from the heat.

CONTINUED

7. When the squash is finished, use a fork to pull away the stringy flesh, and transfer it to serving plates.

8. Sprinkle the squash with the pine nuts, and spoon the sage brown butter on top. Enjoy warm.

NOTE: To cut down on prep time, cook the squash in the microwave. Using a fork, poke several holes in the skin. Using a paring knife, cut slits in the squash where you plan to cut it in half. Microwave on high for 3 minutes. Cut the squash in half, and discard the seeds. Place, cut-side down, in a casserole dish with ½ inch of water. Microwave on high for 6 to 10 minutes, or until tender.

# Pumpkin Marinara Sauce

**MAKES ABOUT 5 CUPS** / **PREP TIME:** 5 minutes / **COOK TIME:** 15 minutes

*Though some people think of their first pumpkin spice latte as the kickoff to fall, in my eyes, the first time I make a batch of this pumpkin sauce signals the start of the season. With pumpkin puree, cinnamon, and honey, it has the beloved creamy texture and subtle sweetness that's characteristic of pumpkin-based desserts but with a unique twist from tomato sauce and oregano.*

**1 tablespoon extra-virgin olive oil**

**1 sweet onion, diced**

**2 cups Homemade Tomato Sauce** (page 251)

**1 (15-ounce) can pumpkin puree**

**1 tablespoon honey**

**½ teaspoon dried oregano**

**½ teaspoon ground cinnamon**

**Salt**

1. In a large saucepan, warm the olive oil over medium heat.

2. Add the onion, and cook for 3 to 4 minutes, or until softened.

3. Stir in the tomato sauce, pumpkin puree, honey, oregano, and cinnamon. Simmer for about 10 minutes, or until the sauce is warmed through and at your desired consistency. Season with salt to taste. Remove from the heat.

**NOTE:** To make homemade pumpkin puree, roast diced pumpkin according to the directions for roasting squash, on page 264. Transfer the roasted pumpkin to a food processor, and pulse until very smooth. Use 2 cups in place of the canned pumpkin for this recipe. If you don't have homemade tomato sauce on hand, you can use 1 (15-ounce) can tomato sauce.

# Acorn Squash with Cranberry and Wild Rice Stuffing

**SERVES 4** / **PREP TIME:** 15 minutes / **COOK TIME:** 45 to 50 minutes

*I had never cooked with wild rice until I moved to Minnesota, where it is the official state grain. Now, I can't get enough of this nutty, protein-rich grain that pairs especially well with acorn squash. With bright red cranberries and green sage, this recipe for stuffed squash can serve as a festive vegetarian main dish for Thanksgiving or Christmas.*

### FOR THE SQUASH

**2 acorn squash, halved
  lengthwise and seeded**
**1 teaspoon olive oil**
**Salt**
**Freshly ground
  black pepper**

### FOR THE STUFFING

**1 cup wild rice**
**3 cups vegetable broth**
**1 tablespoon extra-virgin
  olive oil**
**1 yellow onion, diced**
**1 pound cremini
  mushrooms,
  thinly sliced**
**1 cup fresh cranberries**
**2 tablespoons chopped
  fresh sage**
**½ cup crumbled
  vegetarian feta cheese**

### TO MAKE THE SQUASH

1. Preheat the oven to 400°F. Line a baking sheet with parchment paper.

2. Brush the cut sides of the squash with the olive oil. Season with salt and pepper.

3. Place the squash, cut-sides down, on the prepared baking sheet.

4. Transfer the baking sheet to the oven and bake for 30 to 35 minutes, or until the squash is tender. Remove from the oven.

### TO MAKE THE STUFFING

5. While the squash is roasting, in a saucepan, combine the wild rice and broth. Bring to a boil over high heat.

6. Reduce the heat to medium-low. Cover with a loose-fitting lid and simmer for 25 to 35 minutes, or until the rice is tender. Remove from the heat.

7. In a large skillet, warm the olive oil over medium heat.

8. Add the onion and mushrooms. Cook for 6 to 8 minutes, or until softened.

9. Add the cranberries and sage. Cook for 5 minutes, or until the cranberries begin to pop. Remove from the heat.

10. Stir in the cooked wild rice.

11. Stuff each roasted squash half with a generous spoonful of the stuffing.

12. Sprinkle the stuffed squash with the feta cheese before serving.

NOTE: Some varieties of wild rice take longer to cook, so refer to the package instructions before making it. Cook the rice in advance to cut down on prep time. If you can't find fresh cranberries, substitute ½ cup dried cranberries.

# Zucchini and Yellow Summer Squash

**Season:** summer

**Flavor profile:** With a fairly bland flavor and spongy flesh, zucchini and yellow squash absorb seasonings very well. Their sweet and floral undertones are very subtle.

**Pairs with:** tomatoes, eggplant, garlic, onions, basil, oregano, cheese, soy sauce, red pepper flakes, ginger, chocolate, bananas, oats

**Varieties:** green zucchini, yellow crookneck, pattypan, and several others

**Preparation:** Trim the stems and ends. Use a swivel peeler to remove the skin if desired. Cut into desired size, or run through a spiralizer.

**Favorite ways to serve:** sautéed, roasted, made into noodles, shredded into baked goods

**Nutritional info:** Summer squashes are low in calories but high in water and fiber. Adding them to your diet can help promote healthy digestion.

**Selection:** Choose zucchini and summer squash that are firm, bright in color, and free of scratches. The skin should not be shriveled or spotted.

**Storage:** Put whole, unwashed zucchini in a perforated plastic bag in the produce drawer of the refrigerator. They can be stored for up to two weeks.

# Grilled Zucchini or Yellow Squash

**SERVES 4 TO 6** / **PREP TIME:** 5 minutes / **COOK TIME:** 10 minutes

¼ cup extra-virgin olive oil

4 garlic cloves, minced

4 zucchini or summer
squash, cut into thin,
long strips

Salt

Freshly ground
black pepper

1. Preheat the grill on medium-high heat.

2. In a small bowl, whisk together the olive oil and garlic.

3. Brush each strip of zucchini with the mixture on both sides. Season with salt and pepper.

4. Place the zucchini directly on the grill or on a vegetable mat on the grill. Cook for 3 to 5 minutes on each side, or until tender and slightly charred. Remove from the heat.

# Parmesan-Roasted Zucchini Rounds

**SERVES 4** / **PREP TIME:** 5 minutes / **COOK TIME:** 20 minutes

*Zucchini's mild flavor allows for endless opportunities in the kitchen, but roasting it with a thin layer of salty parmesan is probably my favorite way to enjoy it. With only two main ingredients and 20 minutes in the oven, this simple side dish takes away the stress of prepping vegetables for dinner on a busy evening. It tastes especially delicious on the side with or mixed into pasta.*

**2 zucchini, cut into ½-inch-thick slices**

**½ cup freshly grated vegetarian parmesan cheese**

**Freshly ground black pepper**

1. Preheat the oven to 400°F. Line a baking sheet with parchment paper.

2. Arrange the zucchini in a single layer on the prepared baking sheet.

3. Sprinkle the parmesan cheese onto each zucchini. Season with pepper.

4. Transfer the baking sheet to the oven, and bake for 15 to 20 minutes, or until the cheese has melted and the zucchini is soft. Remove from the oven.

**NOTE:** Substitute other types of summer squash for zucchini in this recipe. This dish is best enjoyed immediately.

# Summer Squash Noodle Salad with Soy-Ginger Vinaigrette

**SERVES 4 TO 6 / PREP TIME:** 15 minutes

*Zucchini and summer squash were the headliners of the spiralized vegetable trend, mainly because their firm but spongy texture makes it really easy to run them through a spiralizer. Although squash noodles are often sautéed with garlic and olive oil, I prefer to keep them raw and add a flavorful dressing. This light salad is a good dish for summer gatherings and meals.*

**3 yellow crookneck squash, trimmed and spiralized into noodles**

**1 cup cooked edamame**

**1 cup shredded carrots**

**1 bell pepper, seeded and diced**

**¼ cup chopped fresh cilantro**

**1 tablespoon toasted sesame seeds**

**Soy-Ginger Vinaigrette** (page 137)

1. In a large bowl, mix together the squash, edamame, carrots, bell pepper, cilantro, and sesame seeds.

2. Add the vinaigrette, and toss until evenly coated. Enjoy immediately or keep in the refrigerator for a few hours until serving.

**NOTE:** To make the squash noodles easier to eat, cut them into smaller pieces with kitchen scissors.

# Zucchini Taco Boats

**SERVES 4** / **PREP TIME:** 10 minutes / **COOK TIME:** 40 minutes

*When you're up to your ears in zucchini, this easy recipe is the perfect dinner to make for "Taco Tuesday." Each boat is stuffed with all the best taco fillings: corn, bell pepper, onion, beans, rice, and cheese. You can even eat them with your hands if you're daring enough. I especially like to wash down this delicious dish with a margarita (or two).*

**Nonstick cooking spray**

**4 zucchini, halved lengthwise**

**1 tablespoon extra-virgin olive oil**

**3 garlic cloves, minced**

**1 bell pepper, seeded and diced**

**½ red onion, diced**

**½ cup corn kernels**

**2 teaspoons ground cumin**

**1 teaspoon chili powder**

**1 (15-ounce) can black beans, drained and rinsed**

**1 cup cooked brown rice**

**Salt**

**1 cup shredded vegetarian Mexican cheese**

**Salsa, for serving**

1. Preheat the oven to 400°F. Grease a 9-by-13-inch baking dish.

2. Using a spoon, scoop out the center of each zucchini half to make room for the stuffing.

3. Place the zucchini halves, skin-side down, in the prepared baking dish.

4. In a large skillet, warm the olive oil over medium heat.

5. Add the garlic, bell pepper, and onion. Cook for 3 to 4 minutes, or until softened.

6. Add the corn, cumin, chili powder, beans, and rice. Season with salt. Cook for about 5 minutes, or until warmed through. Remove from the heat.

7. Spoon the filling into the zucchini halves and sprinkle with the cheese.

8. Transfer the baking dish to the oven and roast for 30 minutes, or until the cheese is melted and starting to brown. Remove from the oven.

9. Serve the taco boats with salsa.

**NOTE:** Other possible toppings include Pickled Jalapeños (page 209) and Avocado-Lime Mash (page 29). To make this dish vegan, omit the cheese.

# Chocolate, Peanut Butter, and Zucchini Smoothie

**SERVES 4** / **PREP TIME:** 5 minutes

*Whenever I can figure out how to combine my love for sweets and vegetables in a single recipe, you know it's going to be a good one. With a base of chopped zucchini, bananas, and almond milk, this creamy smoothie is a healthy twist on my favorite combo: chocolate and peanut butter. I enjoy it as a dessert on hot summer evenings, but with so many healthy ingredients, it also makes for a good post-jog snack or addition to breakfast.*

**2 cups chopped zucchini**

**2 frozen bananas**

**2 cups unsweetened almond milk**

**2 tablespoons peanut butter**

**2 tablespoons unsweetened cocoa powder**

In a blender, combine the zucchini, bananas, almond milk, peanut butter, and cocoa powder. Blend until smooth. Add water as needed until the desired consistency is reached.

**NOTE:** Frozen bananas taste best in this smoothie, but if you don't have them, add a few ice cubes before blending to make it cold.

# Zucchini Bread Cookies

**MAKES 24 COOKIES / PREP TIME:** 10 minutes / **COOK TIME:** 30 minutes

*At the end of the summer when I clean out my backyard vegetable beds, I sometimes find a huge hidden zucchini that had some extra time to grow. This pleasant surprise allows me to bake a few loaves of zucchini bread to freeze for later. Eventually I turned my zucchini bread recipe into cookies that are easier to grab and eat on the go. These mildly sweet, chewy cookies pair wonderfully with coffee for a morning snack.*

1½ cups all-purpose flour

1 cup old-fashioned oats

1 teaspoon
   ground cinnamon

½ teaspoon salt

½ teaspoon
   baking powder

¼ teaspoon baking soda

8 tablespoons (1 stick)
   unsalted butter, at
   room temperature

½ cup maple syrup

1 large egg

1 teaspoon vanilla extract

1 heaping cup
   grated zucchini

1. Preheat the oven to 350°F. Line 2 baking sheets with parchment paper.

2. In a medium bowl, mix together the flour, oats, cinnamon, salt, baking powder, and baking soda.

3. In a large bowl, using an electric hand mixer, beat together the butter, maple syrup, egg, and vanilla until combined.

4. Add the dry ingredients to the wet ingredients, and beat until combined.

5. Using a rubber spatula, fold in the zucchini until incorporated.

6. Form balls of about 2 tablespoons of dough and arrange 2 inches apart on the prepared baking sheets.

7. Transfer the baking sheets to the oven and bake for 12 to 14 minutes, or until the cookies are lightly browned on the bottom and edges. For more even cooking, bake only 1 sheet at a time on the center rack of the oven. Remove from the oven.

8. Transfer the cookies to a rack to cool before eating. Store the cookies in an airtight container at room temperature for up to 5 days, or freeze for up to 3 months.

# Measurement Conversions

| VOLUME EQUIVALENTS | U.S. STANDARD | U.S. STANDARD (OUNCES) | METRIC (APPROXIMATE) |
|---|---|---|---|
| LIQUID | 2 tablespoons | 1 fl. oz. | 30 mL |
| | ¼ cup | 2 fl. oz. | 60 mL |
| | ½ cup | 4 fl. oz. | 120 mL |
| | 1 cup | 8 fl. oz. | 240 mL |
| | 1½ cups | 12 fl. oz. | 355 mL |
| | 2 cups or 1 pint | 16 fl. oz. | 475 mL |
| | 4 cups or 1 quart | 32 fl. oz. | 1 L |
| | 1 gallon | 128 fl. oz. | 4 L |
| DRY | ⅛ teaspoon | — | ½ mL |
| | ¼ teaspoon | — | 1 mL |
| | ½ teaspoon | — | 2 mL |
| | ¾ teaspoon | — | 4 mL |
| | 1 teaspoon | — | 5 mL |
| | 1 tablespoon | — | 15 mL |
| | ¼ cup | — | 59 mL |
| | ⅓ cup | — | 79 mL |
| | ½ cup | — | 118 mL |
| | ⅔ cup | — | 156 mL |
| | ¾ cup | — | 177 mL |
| | 1 cup | — | 235 mL |
| | 2 cups or 1 pint | — | 475 mL |
| | 3 cups | — | 700 mL |
| | 4 cups or 1 quart | — | 1 L |
| | ½ gallon | — | 2 L |
| | 1 gallon | — | 4 L |

### OVEN TEMPERATURES

| FAHRENHEIT | CELSIUS (APPROXIMATE) |
|---|---|
| 250°F | 120°C |
| 300°F | 150°C |
| 325°F | 165°C |
| 350°F | 180°C |
| 375°F | 190°C |
| 400°F | 200°C |
| 425°F | 220°C |
| 450°F | 230°C |

### WEIGHT EQUIVALENTS

| U.S. STANDARD | METRIC (APPROXIMATE) |
|---|---|
| ½ ounce | 15 g |
| 1 ounce | 30 g |
| 2 ounces | 60 g |
| 4 ounces | 115 g |
| 8 ounces | 225 g |
| 12 ounces | 340 g |
| 16 ounces or 1 pound | 455 g |

# Index

# About the Author

 **Lizzie Streit, MS, RDN, LD** is a registered dietitian, recipe developer, nutrition writer, and creator of the food blog *It's a Veg World After All*. As a veggie enthusiast, she is devoted to helping others achieve good physical and mental health via the kitchen by embracing vegetables and learning how to cook plant-forward recipes. Originally from Philadelphia, Lizzie is currently located in Minneapolis, where she enjoys exploring the local food scene, frequenting the outdoor trails and lakes, and experimenting with her backyard vegetable garden. To see more of her work, visit ItsaVegWorldAfterAll.com.

CPSIA information can be obtained
at www.ICGtesting.com
Printed in the USA
LVHW021131181120
671926LV00004B/4

9 781647 393335